Careers for Women without College Degrees

Also by the author
THE BLACK WOMEN'S CAREER GUIDE

Careers for Women without College Degrees

BEATRYCE
NIVENS

McGRAW-HILL BOOK COMPANY

New York St. Louis San Francisco Auckland Bogotá Hamburg
London Madrid Mexico Milan Montreal New Delhi Panama
Paris São Paulo Singapore Sydney Tokyo Toronto

1   2   3   4   5   6   7   8   9   FGR   FGR   8   9   2   1   0   9   8

ISBN 0-07-046578-9

Library of Congress Cataloging-in-Publication Data

Nivens, Beatryce.
  Careers for women without college degrees.

Bibliography: p.
  1. Vocational guidance for women—United States.
2. Women—Employment—United States.   3. High school
graduates—Employment—United States. I. Title.
HF5382.5.U5N52   1988   331.7′02′024042   87-36671
ISBN 0-07-046578-9

Book design by Eve Kirch

For my nieces—
Tanya, Crystal, Faith, and Kristel—
May you move onward and upward
toward your selected careers.

Acknowledgments

Without the support and help of the staff and fellows at the Virginia Center for the Creative Arts, this book couldn't have been written. My sincere thanks to all of them.

Special thanks to the Department of Labor, Bureau of Labor Statistics, for their helpful research materials. And thanks to all of the professional associations whose timely materials helped make this book possible.

Thanks to Josephine Standish, Ingrid James, and Rosezetta Johnson who typed the manuscript.

Many thanks to my special friend, Joseph Lyle, whose positive attitude has helped me finish two books.

And special thanks to my mother, Surluta Nivens, who has been inspirational and supportive throughout my writing career.

Contents

Introduction   1

PART ONE

Plotting Your Career to the Top

1. Polish Your Attitude: It's Never Too Late for Success!   7
2. Plotting Your Course: Heading for the Top   16
3. Skills: What Do I Have to Offer the World?   24
4. Interests: Coming to Grips with What's Important   57
5. Plotting a New Career: The Nuts and Bolts of Career
   Planning   63
6. Résumés: Dazzling Your Prospective Employer with
   Your Skills   81
7. Grabbing the Employer's Attention: Developing
   a Surefire Cover Letter   152
8. Getting the Job: Passing the Interview!   160

PART TWO

Bread and Butter Careers for Women without College Degrees

9. High Technology Careers   185

    Computer Service Technicians   185
    Computer Operators   189
    Word Processing Specialists   192

10. Health Careers   197

    Licensed Practical Nurses   197
    Physical Therapist Assistants   201
    Occupational Therapy Assistants   205
    Dental Assistants   208
    Dispensing Opticians   212
    Emergency Medical Technicians   215

11. Creative Careers   219

    Commercial and Graphic Designers   219
    Photographers   222

12. Legal Careers   227

    Legal Assistants   227
    Court Reporters   231

13. Travel Careers   234

    Travel Agents   234

14. Sales Careers   239

    Insurance Agents and Brokers   239
    Real Estate Agents and Brokers   245
    Manufacturer's Salespeople   250

15. Beauty Careers   254

    Cosmetologists   254

16. Leisure Careers   258

    Hotel and Motel Assistants   258

17. An Entrepreneurial Career 262

    Starting a Business 262

PART THREE

Getting That Sheepskin

18. Going or Returning to College 271

    Junior and Community Colleges 272

    Colleges and Universities 277

    Correspondence Schools and Independent Study 280

    College Credit by Examination 281

    Regents College Examinations (RCEs) 281

    College-Level Examination Program (CLEP) 282

    Graduate Record Examination (GRE) 282

    Defense Activity for Non-Traditional Education
       Support (DANTES) 282

    University End-of-Course Examinations 283

    Regents College Degrees 283

    Thomas A. Edison College 285

    Credit for Noncollege Learning 286

    Credit for Experience 286

    Career Development Women's Studies 287

Appendix A Other Jobs for Women without
       College Degrees 289

Appendix B More Jobs for Women without Degrees 301

Appendix C Women's Business Organizations 305

Suggested Reading 307

Index 313

Figures, Tables, and Worksheets

Worksheet 1	I'm Getting My Life Together	17
Worksheet 2	The Name of the Game Is Money: Making It and Spending It	22
Worksheet 3	What Are My Skills?	25
Worksheet 4	Recognizing Skills	37
Table 1	Skills for a Secretary	38
Table 2	Skills for an Administrative Assistant	41
Table 3	Skills for a Typist	44
Table 4	Skills for a File Clerk	45
Table 5	Skills for an Office Helper	47
Table 6	Skills for a Sales Clerk	49
Table 7	Skills for a Fund-Raiser	51
Table 8	Skills for a Public Relations Specialist	53
Table 9	Do My Interests Have Career Potential?	59
Worksheet 5	Industry Selection	67
Worksheet 6	Networking and Follow-Through Log	73
Figure 1	How to Set Up a Fact-Finding Interview	75
Table 10	Questions to Ask on a Fact-Finding Interview	77

Worksheet 7	Remembering: Preliminary Résumé Analysis	82
Figure 2	Chronological Résumé	103
Figure 3	Functional Résumé	105
Figure 4	Combination Résumé	108
Figure 5	Skeleton Chronological Résumé	112
Figure 6	Résumé Action Words	114
Figure 7	Stress Duties and Skills: "Before" Résumé	118
Figure 8	Stress Duties and Skills: "After" Résumé	120
Figure 9	Focus on Results: "Before" Résumé	122
Figure 10	Focus on Results: "After" Résumé	124
Figure 11	Limit to Relevant Data: "Before" Résumé	128
Figure 12	Limit to Relevant Data: "After" Résumé	130
Figure 13	Changing Fields: "Before" Résumé	132
Figure 14	Changing Fields: "After" Résumé	134
Figure 15	Elaborate on Your Skills: "Before" Résumé	137
Figure 16	Elaborate on Your Skills: "After" Résumé	138
Figure 17	Emphasize Professional Duties: "Before" Résumé	141
Figure 18	Emphasize Professional Duties: "After" Résumé	142
Table 11	Résumé Checklist	144
Worksheet 8	Résumé Analysis Worksheet	149
Figure 19	Referral Cover Letter	154
Figure 20	Response-to-Posting or Want-Ad Cover Letter	156
Figure 21	Sample Cover Letter	158
Table 12	Frequently Asked Interview Questions	161
Table 13	Reasons People Do Not Get Jobs	174
Table 14	Interview Dos and Don'ts	175
Figure 22	Real Estate Specialties	246

Introduction

Suppose you read the following want ad in your Sunday newspaper.

Wanted: Woman without college degree. Must be timid, lacking in self-confidence, and unsure of her skills or work accomplishments. Must be willing to take any job, because she feels worthless without a college degree. Must listen to and believe others who belittle her. Must type, answer phones, make coffee, do any errand. Must be willing to start at the bottom of the salary scale, never hoping to make a decent salary. No creative, self-assured, self-confident women need apply. Only those unwilling to believe in themselves.

You would be angry and hurt and bent on revenge against the company that placed that ad. Yet you may feel and act the way the ad describes. Without a college degree, you may feel doomed and worthless. And everyday someone reminds you of this. It could be your boss, family, coworker, friend, husband or mate, or a host of other doomsayers who get pleasure in putting you down.

Wake up. Just because you didn't go to or complete college, all is not hopeless. You are probably very talented and can improve your lot in life with a little help and direction.

First of all, remember that you are part of a majority. A recent

Department of Commerce Census Bureau study confirmed that 86 percent of all adults over the age of twenty-five in this country are high school graduates, and about 32 percent of the population have some college education.

Second, many top businesswomen have had only a few years of college or no college education at all. Mary Kay Ash of Mary Kay Cosmetics; Lillian Katz of Lillian Vernon; Debbi Fields of Mrs. Fields' Cookies; June Morris of Morris Travel; June Giugni of Cosmetiques; Marilyn Lewis of Hamburger Hamlet; Sybil Ferguson of Diet Center,...and there are many more.

In my seven years of working with women without college degrees, I have seen many go on to satisfying and well-paying careers. A few years ago, I developed a system to help these women look at their on-the-job skills, transferable skills, paid and unpaid work, and interests and see themselves in a new light. Once my clients were in touch with their real "work selves," they were better able to assess themselves, and move into better careers.

Careers for Women without College Degrees will help you get in touch with yourself and your true career goals. You'll stop letting others tell you what's best for you and start making your own career decisions. You'll learn to set monetary goals and to achieve them, too.

In Chapter 3, you'll discover your skills. But more importantly, you'll learn never to downgrade your skills again. At seminars, I often tell people that even the simple task of answering the telephone requires the use of several marketable skills. For example, a receptionist is being an ambassador for her company. If you don't believe it, remember the last time you called a company and someone disagreeable answered the phone. What did you think of that company? Did you want to call back or do business with it? The answer is probably no.

Here are more skills used in answering the telephone: the ability to communicate orally; a pleasant personality; the ability to properly take messages, file messages in the correct box, and give messages promptly; the ability to screen calls and to handle more than one call at a busy company; knowledge about the company and the people who work there; and so on. As you can see from the one job duty of answering the telephone, there can be many skills required to perform it. And this is true of other jobs and job duties.

But why do you need to know this? You are probably working "out of title," that is, you are actually doing more complicated job duties than your job title indicates. You can discover this by doing the skills-analysis exercises in Chapter 3. Your new knowledge will help boost your confidence and keep you from proclaiming, "Who me? I have no skills." And you can take this information and get a raise or a promotion or change careers. This system works for those with paid as well as unpaid (volunteer) work experience.

Chapter 4 will help you analyze your interests and determine careers and/or businesses to which you can transfer your skills from various interests. For example, perhaps you like to cook. Maybe you can turn that interest into a catering business or chef's position. Does flower arranging interest you? Then perhaps turn that into a profitable career or business.

Once you understand yourself better, you will be ready to begin the core work of career planning: looking for a new position with the new you in mind. You'll learn to research your prospective career and industry, go on fact-finding interviews, size up the traditional and nontraditional ways of looking for a job, write a dynamic résumé and cover letter, and win at interviewing and salary negotiations.

Part Two of the book, Bread and Butter Careers for Women without College Degrees, explores nineteen careers: computer science technicians, computer operators, word processing specialists, physical therapy assistants, dental assistants, opticians, emergency medical technicians, commercial artists, photographers, legal assistants, court reporters, travel agents, insurance agents and brokers, real estate agents and brokers, manufacturing sales people, cosmetologists, and hotel and motel managers and assistants. These careers represent those with the best occupational outlooks throughout the 1990s. In addition, Chapter 17 discusses the how-tos of business ownership, essential information if you decide to become self-employed. Finally, Appendixes A and B list other jobs for women without college degrees. To successfully prepare for some of these careers, you may need some training. But other positions require no advance training. You'll explore what each career is like, educational and training requirements, job outlook, related professional associations, salary information, and skills needed for each field.

In Part Three you'll see that it's never too late to get a college degree. There are several programs, both traditional and nontraditional, that are designed to accommodate the older, returning student's special needs. Some of these programs require classroom study; others are a combination of classroom study and various nontraditional methods of getting a degree.

After reading *Careers for Women without College Degrees*, I hope that your life will change for the better. It is no longer necessary to sit on valuable skills because you feel life is hopeless without a college education. Look up as high as you can, and move into a better job. Move on to a better life.

PART ONE

Plotting Your Career to the Top

1

Polish Your Attitude:
It's Never Too Late
for Success!

Aim high. The higher you aim, the more you'll achieve. Perhaps you are very unhappy with your life and job. You feel forever trapped in your job because you don't have a college degree. You have bought the idea that we live in a degree-conscious society, so you feel locked into an unfulfilling job and life. You feel branded for life, cast into hopelessness. You believe that you can't get a better job because you don't have the necessary credentials to move ahead. So you fume and wait for retirement, giving most of your life away to an undesirable job.

You would probably like to have a better job, home, car, and lifestyle but just don't know how to start. This book will show you how to change your life and start moving toward a better job. First, you must clear away the cobwebs that clutter your mind. You must believe in yourself and your achievements. You *must* feel that you can become a better person and get a better job.

It's not easy to destroy years of conditioning. Everyone tells you that you can't do any better. The nonbelievers in your life say that because you didn't go to college you're doomed. Fortunately, nothing can be further from the truth. Once you change your attitude and learn to assess your true skills and abilities, you can and will move up the ladder to success. You won't have to do anything fancy. All you have to do is to be willing to change, be capable of assessing your skills and abilities, and be able to move on.

Let me introduce you to several women who didn't have college degrees but were able to move their lives forward. All of their stories are real, but some of their identities are disguised to protect their privacy. Only they will recognize themselves. Yet you will gain a great deal from their career experiences.

First, let's look at Carolyn McPhearson, an administrative assistant who has an interest in public relations. Like a typical woman without a college degree, she was sitting on many skills and abilities but wasn't in touch with them. She had just enrolled in college hoping to get a degree and then go on to graduate school. Unfortunately, Carolyn didn't realize that she already possessed the skills and experience to land a public relations job.

As a community worker and member of several organizations, she had worked in various public relations capacities. She had developed public relations campaigns, designed and sent out fliers, and so forth.

During a workshop, I asked Carolyn what her skills were. At first, she was stumped. Like many women without college degrees, she had assumed that her skills were very limited. But with my urging, she rattled off five or six very typical "secretarial skills": typing, answering the phone, supervising a secretary, and so on.

She didn't include her community-related public relations skills. When I pointed this out, she said that she wasn't paid for the public relations work, and, she said, unpaid work skills weren't marketable.

Later I asked Carolyn to do a skills-analysis exercise and include her unpaid public relations skills. She was astounded at the large number of public relations skills she had gained. Did it matter that these skills were acquired through unpaid work? Didn't she still have these skills regardless of the way they had been acquired? Couldn't she still perform public relations duties? Couldn't she put these skills to work in a public relations position?

I helped Carolyn rework her résumé to highlight only her public relations skills. I then sent her on several fact-finding interviews. Carolyn had identified people in her prospective field with whom to interview. One of the people Carolyn chose was a public relations director at a large metropolitan transportation agency.

The public relations director was very impressed with Carolyn's knowledge of public relations and particularly her public relations skills. Shortly thereafter, Carolyn received a call from a congressman's office asking her to come interview for a public relations position (she's sure the public relations director recommended her). The position entails handling some of the congressman's public relations duties. Although it's initially an unpaid position, eventually Carolyn can move into a paid position. Until then, she can keep her full-time job and still gain valuable public relations skills during her evenings and weekends at the congressman's office.

Carolyn didn't do anything difficult. She just realized her skills, learned about her prospective field, and marketed herself properly. By changing her attitude about herself and her unpaid public relations skills and prior community experience, she was able to change her life.

Now, let's look at Claudia Powell, who is also an administrative assistant. Like Carolyn, she wasn't in touch with her skills. In fact, she told me, "I really don't have any skills." She also didn't know what she wanted to do with her life. She was getting married soon and moving to another country with her new husband. But she didn't know what type of career to pursue in her future husband's country.

I asked Claudia to look at her job-related skills. Her job title was administrative assistant, but her job duties entailed purchasing for her department. Although her title didn't reflect her true job duties, she learned that her work could primarily be classified as purchasing. More importantly, she liked the purchasing aspects of her job, and purchasing is a marketable skill that can be transferred to work in another country.

Claudia also realized that she had taken courses in purchasing-related areas. As a member of the Army Reserves, she had taken several courses to become a supply sergeant. She loved those courses and the purchasing work she had done for the Army Reserves.

With purchasing skills and training in mind, she redid her résumé to highlight her purchasing and sent it to a city governmental agency that does purchasing for many agencies. Someday she hopes to use her purchasing expertise as a purchasing agent at this agency and ultimately for one of the hotels in her future husband's country.

Carolyn and Claudia aren't any different from you. Because of circumstances beyond their control, they were unable to go to college directly from high school. They married and had children. They were able to accumulate a wide range of skills in their paid and unpaid jobs, and accomplished a great deal. Yet they didn't realize their impressive skills. They were mentally locked into their job titles. But once they realized their true skills, they were able to move their lives forward.

Now, let me introduce you to some other women who have successfully made career progress despite the fact that they don't have college degrees. Some of them have a few years of college. A couple of them have no college education at all.

Irene Gandy is an entertainment publicist. She has worked with major Broadway shows like "Sweet Charity," "Me and My Girl," "I'm Not Rappaport," "Raisin," "Dames at Sea," "Fifth of July," "Purlie," and so on. She has also worked for such entertainers as LaBelle (the now-defunct women's singing group of the seventies), the late Minnie Riperton, Earth Wind and Fire, and others. After high school, her sights were set on an acting career, but she was introduced to theatrical publicity. Excited by the challenge, she apprenticed for three years with a theater press agent and subsequently became a member of the Association of Theatrical Press Agents and Managers.

As a theatrical publicist, she uses publicity to create excitement and ultimately patronage for a theatrical production. For example, a well-placed newspaper article about a show can generate a large audience. Or an interview with a Broadway star can pique interest in a show.

Gandy advises that there are no general prerequisites or training required for the field, but an apprenticeship and union membership is a plus.

Hope E. Daley began her post–high school years studying to become a news reporter at the State University of New York at New Paltz. But many people gave her discouraging news about employment and turnover in the field. After two years of study, she came home one Christmas break and began doing temporary work at Morgan Stanley, an investment banking firm.

She loved the corporate environment and decided to stay. She let people know that she wanted a permanent, full-time position with the company. The company soon offered her a position of call director at an annual salary of $13,500. In this position, she answered telephones, screened calls, and forwarded messages to those in the international department.

After one year, she was promoted to the position of secretary to the office manager in investment banking. There, she learned about personnel matters and helped handle various administrative duties.

When Morgan Stanley became public, a reorganization created slots for office managers on each of the investment banking floors. Hope was offered one of these positions. Today, at twenty-five, she is office manager and trainer and works for various departments like international banking, merchant banking, and leverage buy-outs. She is responsible for the day-to-day issues involving employee problems, compensation, temporary replacement of secretaries who are sick or on vacation, recruiting and hiring, and helping with space planning.

One of her pet projects is the training program for entry-level secretaries. Women with no real work experience are hired and given training in telephone techniques, secretarial duties, company history, and so on. Hope developed the training manual for the program and trains the participants. She also frequently gives lectures to students in secretarial schools.

Her advice to women without college degrees is to "reach for the stars." And she is currently doing just that. With more focus and direction this time, she has returned to school to complete a degree.

Rose TenEyck's career strategies have landed her in a top position as national sales manager for KGO NewsTalk Radio in San Francisco, California. Rose attended Nassau Community College and Hofstra University. A position at Dancer and Fitzgerald, an advertising agency, started her on the path to her present job. While at the advertising agency, she landed a position in media research, and was introduced to broadcast sales. The broadcast sales staff bought time for advertisements on radio and television, and this business intrigued her. She wanted to move into the area, but knew that a unique career planning approach was needed. She couldn't very easily move from one field to the other. So, she took a research directorship at a small radio representative firm. Some of her duties include getting advertising agencies from across the country to buy radio time.

Ultimately, she applied for a research position at a radio station, KGO. Her dream was to get into sales, and this move helped accomplish this. As research director, she was in close contact with the salespeople, providing them with research materials to make sales presentations, and even going out on client calls with them. Two years later, she moved into her dream job in sales for ABC Radio Spot Sales, ABC's in-house national FM-radio representative firm. Later, she returned to KGO as an account executive. After several years, she was promoted to national sales manager for the radio station.

Rose, who credits her success to her strong writing skills, believes it would not be so easy for women to obtain her position without a college degree. But if one is willing to work in a small market, there can be possibilities in broadcast sales.

Susan Taylor zoomed to the top of her field with talent, brains, creativity, and most importantly, spirituality. This editor in chief of *Essence*, vice president of Essence Communications, and host and executive producer for "Essence," a weekly syndicated television show, did this feat without a college degree. At first, she wanted to become an actress, but the birth of her daughter made her focus on another field. She became a cosmetologist and also started one of the first black cosmetics companies, Nequai Cosmetics.

She soon learned that the beauty editor's position at *Essence* was available, and she was hired for that position as a free-lancer. Shortly thereafter, she became the magazine's editor for the fashion and beauty department. As the magazine grew, Susan's vision of her fashion and beauty department grew with a unique approach.

When the editor in chief's position became available, publisher Ed Lewis turned to Susan to take the lead. Under her guidance, the magazine now boasts a circulation of 850,000 subscriptions and a readership of 4 million on a monthly basis. And Susan has become the most powerful black woman in communications.

Susan, who believes strongly in education, has decided to pursue a degree at Fordham University and, in fact, has appeared in advertisements for them.

Her schedule is hectic, but she has an abundance of time to be a loving mother to daughter Shana. She also has time for lecturing to groups across the country. How does she do it all? Her spirituality gives her a powerful base, and she reflects this power through her monthly "In the Spirit" columns for *Essence*. Susan Taylor is a role model for all women who aim high!

Lisa Cohen is a second vice president for a large midwestern bank. Originally, she wanted to become an actress, singer, and model, and dabbled in those fields. While pursuing these careers, she took a job as a waitress in a chic restaurant, and hoped for her lucky break. Discouraged that the breaks weren't coming fast enough, she decided to go to college. She enrolled as a liberal arts major at a small junior college. After almost two years of study, she wanted to get a full-time job and have the company pay for her education.

Lisa knew someone who was working in personnel at a bank, and she dropped off her résumé. Within weeks, she was hired as a research coordinator in the bank's public relations department. In this position, she kept up with the news, and routed articles to the bank's senior executives.

In three years, she was promoted to assistant treasurer in the division and added budget matters and budget control to her responsibilities. Two years later, she was promoted to second vice president of the public relations division.

She reports directly to the senior vice president in charge of public relations and supervises the entire secretarial staff. She also manages a $5 million budget, including helping her boss decide who in the division is due a raise, and what kind. And she oversees all personnel matters for the eight-department division.

Her public relations division is responsible for enhancing the bank's image to the media and the public. They also are responsible for the bank's annual and quarterly reports, publications (both internal and external), archives, neighborhood grants, philanthropic activities (the millions of dollars given away to worthy organizations and causes), speech writing for the chairman and other senior executives, and so on.

Cohen gives this advice to women without college degrees: "I'm a hands-on person and have learned a great deal this way. If you're smart, have common sense, and have done well in English, you should be able to do well in many careers. Many of the jobs do not require a college degree. But you must believe in yourself and your abilities. That coupled with some experience is a winning combination." Good advice from someone who is obviously winning in her career.

These women are representative of the thousands of women who have carved impressive careers without the benefit of college degrees. Some of them now see the benefit of returning to school. But the lack of a college degree hasn't hampered them in their trip to success.

Like these women, you can also change your life. You must begin by taking the risk of freeing yourself to experience different possibilities. You must steer your life in a new direction, and take charge.

Many of us feel completely powerless when it comes to positive change. It's so easy to just give up and go deeply into despair. Most people are unhappy with their lives and just give up. But not you!

For today, you have started on a journey to release yourself from the stranglehold of underdevelopment in your career and life. You will be positive about yourself. You will get to know yourself. And you will start making a difference in your life.

After you've read *Careers For Women Without College Degrees,* you will not just say "great book" and put it away to gather dust. You will become inspired to take your place among those precious few who have risen to their highest potential. Tomorrow, you will be glad for the life you have created, and be thankful for your blessings and abilities.

You must have an open mind about yourself and your abilities. Know that all things are possible and that you can achieve. And when you step into that satisfying career, you'll know that you made it to the mountaintop.

2

Plotting Your Course:
Heading for the Top

Today is the beginning of a new you. No longer will you be in search of your destiny. You will carve your own way. Like the captain of a ship, you will carefully maneuver your way through the world of work. You will become empowered by being in charge of your life!

You can begin by taking a long look at you. Roll up your sleeves and start flexing your mental muscles. The first step is deciding on your goals. What are your goals? Every successful person sets and completes goals. Have you thought about yours? Have you thought about what it is that you want out of life? Don't be vague! Some people say they want a lot of money. When asked how they will achieve this, they just shrug their shoulders. Others want large homes, cars, and other luxury items. When asked how they will get these things, their faces become blank. In life few people have achieved things without first establishing a game plan to achieve their dreams.

To have no goals is like going from point A to point B without knowing what point B is. It's virtually impossible. Would you take a plane without knowing the destination and just hope to land where you want to be?

So let's establish your point B before anything else. Where are you going? What do you ultimately want to do? Let's look at Worksheet 1, Question 1. This question will help uncover your real career goal. It helps you get in touch with your real career desires. As a child, these desires were very strong until limitations were placed upon you by adults. How often did your parents or others tell you that you couldn't achieve or enter a certain field?

WORKSHEET 1
I'm Getting My Life Together

1. When you were a child, before limitations were placed on you, what did you want to do?

   _____

2. Now that you are an adult, what is it that you truly want to do? Forget about the limitations! Do some soul-searching and discover your true desires. Be honest.

   _____

   _____

   _____

   _____

3. What are five positive steps you can take to realize your dreams?

   a. _____

   _____

   _____

   b. _____

   _____

   _____

   c. _____

   _____

   _____

d. _____

_____

_____

e. _____

_____

_____

4. What are three possible stumbling blocks that are in the way of your achieving your dreams?

_____

_____

_____

5. If you had complete control over your life, what five things would you do to overcome these stumbling blocks?

a. _____

_____

_____

b. _____

_____

_____

c. _____

_____

_____

d. _____

_____

_____

e. _____

_____

_____

6. When do you want to achieve your goals?

_____

_____

_____

7. What are your short-range (one-day to six-month) goals?

_____

_____

_____

8. What are your medium-range (six-month to five-year) goals?

_____

_____

_____

9. What are your long-range goals?

a. Five years? _____

_____

_____

_____

_____

b. Ten years? _____

_____

_____

_____

_____

Often well-meaning parents, teachers, and relatives don't allow a child's real occupational dreams to blossom. They stifle children's real career dreams in order to protect them and to steer them to other more suitable, secure careers. As a result, you may have stifled your true career dreams and opted for more suitable ones. Settling for what's comfortable has taught you a painful lesson: if you don't work at what you love, you die a little each day.

Every day, clients come to me for career counseling. Most are unhappy with their present jobs or just want to change careers and make more money. Some of them want to be tested for the "right career." After talking with them, I have discovered that most of them already know what it is that they want to do. Under layers and layers of "other people telling them what to do" are their real career dreams. As those real career dreams surface, happy smiles appear on their faces. And slowly, I help them move toward their real career choices.

Forget about your age, ability to pay for additional education, or family or monetary responsibilities. Just focus now on what you truly want to do. Sit back, close your eyes. Remember your childhood. Let happy childhood pictures flash into your mind. Remember things that made you happy. Can you remember what you wanted to be? And why? Jot down those memories!

Question 2 will help you discover that some of your career dreams have changed slightly from childhood. For example, perhaps you wanted to be a nurse as a child. As an adult, you found the sight of blood makes you feel uncomfortable, but you still want to help people. Choose a career that can offer the same rewards as nursing. Remember, put aside the limitations that pop into your mind. Close your eyes and relax for twenty minutes. Imagine yourself doing exactly what you want to do. See yourself working at your ideal profession. Say to yourself, "If I had complete control over my life, this is what I would be doing."

Next, go to Question 3. Write down five positive steps that you can take right now to help you realize those dreams. Do you need to learn more about your chosen career area? For example, you can look up career information at your local library, or talk to a neighbor or friend who is currently employed in your prospective field. Write down five ways that you can start learning more about your chosen career.

Question 4 focuses on possible "stumbling blocks" that may prevent you from achieving your goal. For example, if you are sixty-four years old and always wanted to be a doctor, age may be a factor in terms of realizing your dreams. It doesn't mean that you can't work in the health field—perhaps just not as a physician.

Although many women who answer this question put down age as a stumbling block, this isn't really true in the majority of cases. Remember to change your attitude about age. Remember that many successful people started careers *after* they retired.

Question 5 helps you work on removing these stumbling blocks, most of which are really mental blocks. Freeing yourself of old attitudes will help dissolve most of them.

Now after some soul-searching, you should have some idea what you want to do. You should also be aware of some of the obstacles and how to overcome them. It's time to set some goals together with timetables. Let's look at Question 6: "When do you want to achieve your goals?" For example, you may say, "I want to be a computer operator." That's a fine goal. Now think about how long it will realistically take you to accomplish this. If you've had no computer training and can only go to school part-time, think of how long it will take you to accomplish your goal. One year? Two years or more? Be more specific! Write down the exact date that you plan to achieve your goal. Perhaps it's December 30, 1995.

Sometimes, the simple size of our goals can overwhelm us, and as a result our goals are never achieved. To avoid this, break your goals into small, manageable parts: short-term, medium-range, and long-range. If you work on small manageable goals, you are more likely to accomplish them. Questions 7 and 8 will help you determine your short- and medium-range goals. Question 9 will help you project long-range goals: five- and ten-year goals. If you can't look that far into the future, that's fine. Just focus on the short- and medium-range goals. In time, you will be able to make long-range goals. Remember, goal setting is a lifelong process. It doesn't all have to be done in one sitting.

It is very important to also have monetary goals. You may work for the satisfaction of your job, but you also want some monetary rewards for your endeavors. Worksheet 2 helps you decide your monetary goals. You may wonder why it's important to write down monetary goals. Like career goals, monetary goals are almost impossible to achieve without knowing what it is you want. Just wanting more money isn't specific enough! How much do you want? $5,000? $10,000? $25,000? A million dollars?

WORKSHEET 2
The Name of the Game Is Money:
Making It and Spending It

1. What amount of money do you want to make in one year?

_____

2. What amount do you want to make in five years?

_____

3 a. What amount of money do you want to make in ten years (for the ambitious money-goal-setters)?

_____

   b. Fifteen years (for the ambitious money-goal-setters)?

_____

4 a. In what five ways can you achieve your monetary goals? Do some deep thinking. How can you realistically increase your monetary rewards in the next year?

_____

_____

_____

_____

   b. In the next five years? _____

_____

_____

_____

_____

c. In the next ten years? _____

_____

_____

_____

_____

5 **a.** If you are an ambitious big thinker, project your monetary goals further into the future. In what five ways can you achieve your goals in the next fifteen years?

_____

_____

_____

_____

b. In the next twenty-five years? _____

_____

_____

_____

_____

Questions 1 through 4 in this worksheet help you decide your monetary goals for one, five, and ten years. If you're ambitious, make fifteen- and twenty-five–year money goals. Then decide exactly how to make the money you want. For example, your monetary goal may be to make $5,000 more in the next year. How can you achieve this? One way is to get one or two raises. Maybe you can think of something you did for your company that merits a raise. Did you, for instance, develop a filing system that increased office productivity by 65 percent? If so, does your supervisor know about it? If not, tell him or her. You may just merit a raise or bonus. Do a little thinking and figuring. Determine how you can meet your monetary goals within the next year or next five or ten years.

3

Skills: What Do I Have to Offer the World?

Since you now know your goals, let's see what skills you have with which to accomplish them. What are skills? Many people are thrown by the word. Skills are simply things that you do well. You have skills that are God-given, such as singing or creative writing. You have skills received from school, such as in math or spelling. You have skills that you received from paid employment, such as secretarial or administrative abilities. You have skills from parenting, such as nurturing, and those learned from being a homemaker, such as food management and budgeting. And you have skills from your unpaid community or civic work, such as organizing or public relations.

Skills are troubling because most of us don't know how to determine them. Ask a typical secretary, for example, what her skills are, and she will probably say, "typing and answering the telephone." But if we look carefully at a secretary's work, we will see that she does much more. Some secretaries wear several hats, as managers, purchasing agents, salespeople, and a variety of other roles.

Like the typical secretary, most of us view our jobs narrowly. Yet, most of us know that we are working out of title or well beyond our job description. We are also using skills beyond those job titles! But how do you begin to get in touch with your various skills? You begin by looking at a list of skills and checking off those skills you have.

Look at Worksheet 3. On the left, you'll see a list of skills. In the first column, check off your skills from paid work experience. In the middle column, check off the skills you have from unpaid work experience (volunteer, community, church, or civic work).

WORKSHEET 3
What Are My Skills?

Skills	Skills from paid work	Skills from unpaid work	Skills I would like to use in my future career
Abstracting			
Accommodating			
Accomplishing			
Accounting			
Acting			
Activating			
Adapting			
Addressing			
Adjusting			
Administering			
Advertising			
Advising			
Advocating			
Allocating			

(continued)

WORKSHEET 3 (*Continued*)

Skills	*Skills from paid work*	*Skills from unpaid work*	*Skills I would like to use in my future career*
Analyzing			
Anticipating			
Appraising			
Approving			
Arranging			
Artistry			
Assembling			
Asserting			
Assessing			
Assigning			
Auditing			
Balancing			
Bargaining			
Bookkeeping			
Brainstorming			
Budgeting			
Building			
Calculating			
Caring			
Cataloging			
Catering			
Changing			

WORKSHEET 3 (*Continued*)

Skills	Skills from paid work	Skills from unpaid work	Skills I would like to use in my future career
Classifying			
Coaching			
Collaborating			
Collecting			
Combining			
Committee working			
Communicating			
Comparing			
Compiling			
Composing			
Computing			
Conceiving			
Conducting			
Constructing			
Consulting			
Contracting			
Contributing			
Controlling			
Cooking			
Cooperating			
Coordinating			
Copying			

(*continued*)

WORKSHEET 3 (*Continued*)

Skills	*Skills from paid work*	*Skills from unpaid work*	*Skills I would like to use in my future career*
Counseling			
Counting			
Creating			
Critiquing			
Dancing			
Debating			
Deciding			
Decorating			
Defining			
Delegating			
Delivering			
Demonstrating			
Designing			
Detailing			
Detecting			
Determining			
Developing			
Devising			
Diagnosing			
Directing			
Disciplining			
Discovering			

WORKSHEET 3 (*Continued***)**

Skills	Skills from paid work	Skills from unpaid work	Skills I would like to use in my future career
Discussing			
Dispensing			
Displaying			
Distributing			
Drafting			
Drawing			
Editing			
Educating			
Encouraging			
Enduring			
Enforcing			
Enlarging			
Enlisting			
Entertaining			
Establishing			
Estimating			
Evaluating			
Examining			
Exercising			
Exhibiting			
Expanding			
Expediting			

(continued)

WORKSHEET 3 (*Continued*)

Skills	Skills from paid work	Skills from unpaid work	Skills I would like to use in my future career
Experimenting			
Explaining			
Exploring			
Expressing			
Facilitating			
Feeding			
Filing			
Finding			
Fixing			
Following through			
Forecasting			
Formulating			
Fund-raising			
Gathering			
Governing			
Graphing			
Group facilitating			
Guiding			
Handling			
Handling complaints			
Handling detail work			
Helping			

WORKSHEET 3 (*Continued*)

Skills	Skills from paid work	Skills from unpaid work	Skills I would like to use in my future career
Identifying			
Imagining			
Implementing			
Improving			
Indexing			
Initiating			
Innovating			
Inspecting			
Inspiring			
Instructing			
Interpreting			
Interviewing			
Inventing			
Investigating			
Judging			
Justifying			
Laboratory working			
Leading			
Learning			
Lecturing			
Listening			
Lobbying			

(*continued*)

WORKSHEET 3 (Continued)

Skills	Skills from paid work	Skills from unpaid work	Skills I would like to use in my future career
Locating			
Maintaining			
Making layouts			
Making models			
Managing			
Manipulating			
Mapping			
Measuring			
Mechanical reasoning			
Mediating			
Meeting the public			
Memorizing			
Moderating			
Modifying			
Monitoring			
Motivating oneself			
Motivating others			
Moving with dexterity			
Navigating			
Negotiating			
Nursing			
Observing			

WORKSHEET 3 (*Continued*)

Skills	Skills from paid work	Skills from unpaid work	Skills I would like to use in my future career
Obtaining information			
Operating			
Organizing			
Overseeing			
Painting			
Perceiving			
Performing			
Persevering			
Persuading			
Planning			
Policy making			
Politicking			
Predicting			
Preparing			
Presenting			
Presiding			
Printing			
Prioritizing			
Problem solving			
Processing			
Producing			
Programming			

(*continued*)

WORKSHEET 3 (Continued)

Skills	Skills from paid work	Skills from unpaid work	Skills I would like to use in my future career
Promoting			
Proofreading			
Proposal writing			
Protecting			
Public speaking			
Purchasing			
Reacting			
Reading			
Reasoning			
Recognizing problems			
Recommending			
Reconciling			
Recording			
Record keeping			
Recruiting			
Rectifying			
Reducing costs			
Rehabilitating			
Remembering			
Reorganizing			
Reporting			
Representing			

WORKSHEET 3 (*Continued*)

Skills	Skills from paid work	Skills from unpaid work	Skills I would like to use in my future career
Reproducing			
Researching			
Resolving			
Restoring			
Reviewing			
Rewriting			
Risk taking			
Scanning			
Scheduling			
Screening			
Simplifying			
Singing			
Solving			
Solving quantitative problems			
Speaking			
Stimulating			
Strengthening			
Summarizing			
Supervising			
Systematizing			
Taking shorthand			

(*continued*)

WORKSHEET 3 (*Continued*)

Skills	Skills from paid work	Skills from unpaid work	Skills I would like to use in my future career
Talking			
Targeting			
Teaching			
Team building			
Technical working			
Thinking			
Timing			
Training			
Transmitting			
Treating			
Troubleshooting			
Typing			
Understanding			
Updating			
Using instruments			
Validating			
Visualizing			
Working with others			
Working with precision			
Writing			

There are more than 250 skills listed in the pages of this chart. See how many you have. Remember to include all of your skills. By the end of this chapter, you will find that you have many more than you thought. Next, go back over your list of skills and in the third column check off which ones you want to use in your future career. Be honest and imaginative!

Now that you have made a preliminary assessment of your skills, let's expand your number of skills. Worksheet 4 and Tables 1 through 8 will help. Look at Worksheet 4. On the left, it says, "Job Duties"; on the right, it says, "Skills Required." Each of us can list twenty or more job duties. List yours on Worksheet 4. If you are having trouble, make a daily log of the things you do at work. Jot down everything that you do during the day. If you do this exercise for a month, you will be surprised at the many different types of duties you perform. Remember, forget about your job description—concentrate on what you actually do!

WORKSHEET 4
Recognizing Skills

Job duties	*Skills required*
1._____	1._____
2._____	2._____
3._____	3._____
4._____	4._____
5._____	5._____
6._____	6._____
7._____	7._____
8._____	8._____
9._____	9._____
10._____	10._____
11._____	11._____
12._____	12._____

Now look at Table 1. On the left, it lists the job duties of a secretary. On the right side, it says, "Skills Required." What does this mean? Go back to the example of the secretary who says that her only skills are typing and answering the phone. In order to do each of these tasks, she must use other skills. For example, by answering the telephone she is also being of service to her boss; being diplomatic; being sensitive to others; showing an ability to take messages and give correct and timely messages, being patient and fair, and being a liaison for the company and her boss. So while a secretary may think she has only one or two skills, she really has at least seven or more skills from the one job duty of answering the phones. If she analyzes 20 job duties, she'll probably have as many as 150 or more skills.

TABLE 1
Skills for a Secretary

Job duties	Skills required
1. Relieves executive of various administrative duties.	1. Being of service and being sensitive to boss; able to work under pressure.
2. Coordinates and maintains effective office procedures and efficient work flows.	2. Gets the job done; ability to move others to get the job done, to persuade and to facilitate.
3. Implements policies and procedures set by employer.	3. Is orderly; keeps records; able to process information; can do many tasks.
4. Establishes and maintains harmonious working relationships with superiors, coworkers, subordinates, customers or clients, and suppliers.	4. Takes initiative; has people management skills, relates well to public and fellow employees or boss; has ability to effectively deal with many people.

TABLE 1 (*Continued*)

Job duties	*Skills required*
5. Schedules appointments and maintains calendar.	5. Coordinates; able to persuade when difficulty arises; able to evaluate.
6. Receives and assists visitors and telephone callers and refers them to executive.	6. Diplomatic; sensitive to others; patient and fair; comfortable with many different kinds of people; is liaison for boss and others.
7. Arranges business itineraries and coordinates executive travel requirements.	7. Is helpful; good at organizing details and written material; makes arrangements for others; responsible.
8. Takes action authorized during executive's absence and uses initiative and judgment to see that matters requiring attention are referred to delegated authority or handled in a manner so as to minimize effect of employer's absence.	8. Able to follow through; able to assist and lead in absence of boss; able to assume other duties; able to direct others; able to communicate effectively.
9. Takes and transcribes manual shorthand or transcribes from machine dictation.	9. Able to transcribe and to take shorthand.
10. Types material from longhand or rough copy.	10. Types, analyzes, edits, corrects and obtains information from boss or others to complete the job.

(*continued*)

TABLE 1 (*Continued*)

Job duties	*Skills required*
11. Sorts and reads incoming mail and documents and attaches appropriate file to facilitate necessary action; determines routing and signatures required and maintains follow-up.	11. Able to sort, read, file, and observe; gets the task done; able to do follow-up and detail work.
12. Composes correspondence and reports for own or executive signature.	12. Able to compose letters and write well.
13. Prepares communication outlined by executive in oral or written directions.	13. Able to follow directions.
14. Gathers information from various sources.	14. Able to do research and to get information from others.
15. Schedules conferences and meetings.	15. Schedules, communicates with others, and takes others' plans into consideration.
16. Handles sticky situations with diplomacy.	16. Diplomatic; able to handle difficult situations.
17. Analyzes information.	17. Able to analyze.
18. Has good writing and speaking skills.	18. Speaks and writes well.
19. Saves time for boss and self.	19. Considerate of other people's and self's time.

This chart first appeared in Beatryce Nivens, *The Black Woman's Career Guide*, 1982. Source for job duties: "The Prototypes of Secretarial Policies," National Secretaries Association International, 1974. Source for skills required: U.S. Department of Labor, Bureau of Labor Statistics, 1977, *Dictionary of Occupational Titles*.

Now, go back and look at the skills in Worksheet 3 and try to recognize what skills are required to perform your job duties. This will take a little time, but it's well worth the effort. To help out, there are seven more job duties and skills tables (Tables 2 through 8) for typical jobs held by women without college degrees. Use these tables to help assess your on-the-job and unpaid work skills.

TABLE 2
Skills for an Administrative Assistant

Job duties	*Skills required*
1. Aids executive by coordinating office services such as personnel and budget preparation and control.	1. Is of service to boss; is organized; able to appraise services; plans effectively; can delegate tasks; can do detail work; can initiate; able to manage information and people; is able to obtain information; monitors; able to keep records; can formulate budgets.
2. Studies management methods in order to improve work flow; simplifies reporting procedures or implements cost reductions; analyzes unit operating practices such as record keeping systems; forms control, office layout, suggestion systems, personnel and budgetary requirements, and performance standards to create new systems or revise established procedures.	2. Appraises and evaluates office set-up; researches and investigates; obtains information; interprets facts; compiles facts and statistical data; determines most effective systems to increase office efficiency; designs plan of action; estimates cost of operation; prepares findings for boss; makes recommendations and advises.

(continued)

TABLE 2 (Continued)

Job duties	Skills required
3. Analyzes jobs to define position responsibilities for use in wage and salary adjustments.	3. Reviews and interprets duties for various jobs; classifies; makes decisions about job; examines; estimates salaries; does detail work; monitors; obtains information; does record keeping; is resourceful; updates and improves.
4. Coordinates collection and preparation of operating reports such as time and attendance records, terminations, new hires, transfers, budget expenditures, and statistical records of performance data.	4. Supervises; advises others; compiles statistical information; designs plan that will implement action; explains procedures to others; finds others who can be helpful to project; locates information; is responsible for getting the work done; motivates others to get the job done; persuades.
5. Prepares reports including conclusions and recommendations for solution.	5. Able to write; able to review; analyzes data; interprets and advises in writing to others; observes; reports; compares; summarizes; makes recommendations; able to collect information, compile, and put into a report; makes decisions; able to deal with deadlines and pressure; initiates new ideas.

TABLE 2 (*Continued*)

Job duties	*Skills required*
6. Issues and interprets operating policies.	6. Reviews; able to orally communicate; able to define; able to give directions to others; reports on policies; advises; explains; interprets; able to persuade; represents boss to other employees; teaches.
7. Reviews and answers correspondence.	7. Communicates effectively through writing; able to observe; able to initiate letters; able to edit; able to prioritize; able to make decisions, to evaluate, and to express thoughts in writing.
8. May interview job applicants; direct orientation of new employees.	8. Recruits; able to screen; able to listen; can make decisions; able to use good judgment; evaluates, able to obtain information; able to observe; able to choose; coaches; teaches; able to influence others.
9. May direct services, such as maintenance.	9. Able to supervise; able to make others get the job done; can appraise; can make decisions; able to observe others in the process of performing work tasks.

Source for job duties: U.S. Department of Labor, Bureau of Labor Statistics, 1977, *Dictionary of Occupational Titles.*

TABLE 3
Skills for a Typist

Job duties	*Skills required*
1. Types letters, reports, stencils, forms, addresses, or other straight copy material from rough draft or corrected copy.	1. Applies knowledge of typing and clerical work; being of service to employer; able to type accurately; able to coordinate movement of hands, eyes, and fingers to operate typing machine; has finger dexterity; able to organize materials; able to update and improve; is reliable; has ability to get the job done; able to answer correspondence; can do detail work.
2. May verify totals on report forms, requisitions, or bills.	2. Able to make comparisons; able to add and do other mathematical equations; able to test accuracy; able to make decisions; obtains information; pays attention to details.
3. May operate duplicating machines to reproduce copy.	3. Able to do routine work repeatedly; can follow simple instructions; able to adjust machine for speed, size of paper, and flow of process liquid to moistening pad.

Source for job duties: U.S. Department of Labor, Bureau of Labor Statistics, 1977, *Dictionary of Occupational Titles.*

TABLE 4
Skills for a File Clerk

Job duties	*Skills required*
1. Files correspondence, cards, invoices, receipts.	1. Able to classify and sort, able to determine where material should be placed; able to make decisions; observes; examines, inspects; locates; is patient; uses good judgment; able to concentrate.
2. Reads incoming materials; according to file systems, places material in file cabinets, drawers, or special filing cases.	2. Reviews; able to organize and select appropriate materials; able to appraise situation; classifies; collects; able to make decisions; able to do detail work; is orderly; able to update information in filing system; able to process information.
3. Locates and removes materials.	3. Able to find information; able to observe and inspect; able to select; able to obtain specific information at a minute's notice; able to expedite matters.

(*continued*)

TABLE 4 (*Continued*)

Job duties	*Skills required*
4. Keeps records of material removed; stamps reports received; traces missing file folders; types indexing information on folders.	4. Able to do record keeping; monitors; uses stamping device; investigates; finds and locates; collects material; explains need to locate material to others in department or other departments; able to type information correctly on folders; pays attention to detail; able to update.
5. May enter data on records.	5. Able to write; can summarize; able to update; able to repeat tasks; able to do detail work; can record and review.

Source for job duties: U.S. Department of Labor, Bureau of Labor Statistics, 1977, *Dictionary of Occupational Titles*.

TABLE 5
Skills for an Office Helper

Job duties	Skills required
1. Gives others clerical supplies.	1. Classifies or sorts information; coordinates quantities of information; dispenses; distributes; able to estimate; evaluates; able to follow through on assigned tasks; able to locate supplies; able to prepare; does record keeping.
2. Opens, sorts, and distributes mail.	2. Able to organize; gathers information and arranges it; inspects; reviews mail; able to make a decision; able to concentrate; able to get the job done; selects; is responsible.
3. Collects, seals, and stamps outgoing mail.	3. Able to pay attention to detail; keeps track of mail; able to use envelope-sealing and stamp meter machine; is reliable; inspects; observes; able to put mail in orderly position; able to repeat tasks; reviews.
4. Delivers oral and written messages.	4. Communicates well both verbally and in writing; able to give correct messages; is of service to boss and in office.

(*continued*)

TABLE 5 (*Continued*)

Job duties	*Skills required*
5. Collects and distributes paperwork like records or time cards from one department to another.	5. Able to make decisions; able to obtain information; able to cooperate with others in another department; reliable; able to organize; able to make arrangements for the collection and distribution of paperwork or records.
6. Marks, tabulates, and files articles and records.	6. Able to observe, record, and organize; arranges; reviews; able to decide; uses good judgment; appraises; able to condense; lists.
7. Uses office equipment such as envelope-sealing machine and letter opener.	7. Able to learn equipment and operate properly; is quick learner; able to obtain desired results from equipment.
8. May deliver items to other business establishments.	8. Represents employer to other business establishments; is diplomatic; able to be patient; has a good appearance; able to locate various businesses.

Source for job duties: U.S. Department of Labor, Bureau of Labor Statistics, 1977, *Dictionary of Occupational Titles.*

TABLE 6
Skills for a Sales Clerk

Job duties	*Skills required*
1. Obtains merchandise from customers; totals bills; receives payment; makes change for customers.	1. Able to select or choose; able to sell; is of service to others; able to deal with the public; is diplomatic; is enthusiastic; uses good judgment; has integrity; able to communicate; able to close a deal; can calculate; can do simple mathematical equations; can collect; able to persuade.
2. Stocks shelves, counters, or tables with merchandise.	2. Able to inspect and compare; classifies; makes decisions; locates; able to handle detail work; organizes; able to do inventory.
3. Sets up advertising displays or arranges merchandise on counters or tables to promote sales.	3. Designs; displays; exhibits; predicts; able to promote; can sell; able to persuade and stimulate by utilizing displays; able to organize; is creative; able to create displays based on correct colors, shapes, and products; is visual; able to set up interesting visual displays.
4. Stamps, marks, or tags prices on merchandise.	4. Able to use marking devices; inspects; able to work at a fast pace; pays attention to detail; able to be persistent; can sort; able to deal with pressure; locates; can observe.

(*continued*)

TABLE 6 (*Continued*)

Job duties	*Skills required*
5. Obtains merchandise requested by customers or receives merchandise selected by customers.	5. Able to sell; distributes; able to get the job done; able to follow through; good at listening; can handle difficult people; able to deal with pressure; able to handle complaints.
6. May calculate sales discount in preparing sales slip.	6. Able to add, subtract, and multiply; able to decide feasibility of discount; able to advise supervisor of discount; has listening skills; able to observe.
7. Wraps or bags merchandise for customers.	7. Able to fold or pack correctly; is patient; pays attention to detail.
8. May keep record of sales and prepares inventory of stock or order merchandise.	8. Able to do record keeping; able to log; keeps files and/or file system; able to appraise; observes; estimates; decides; inspects; orders.

Source for job duties: U.S. Department of Labor, Bureau of Labor Statistics, 1977, *Dictionary of Occupational Titles*.

TABLE 7
Skills for a Fund-Raiser

Job duties	*Skills required*
1. Plans fund-raising program for charities or other causes.	1. Has vision; sets goals; is good at exchanging information and making recommendations; can research; can analyze; can review.
2. Writes to, telephones, or visits individuals or establishments to solicit funds and persuades them to contribute funds by explaining purpose and benefits of fund-raising program.	2. Can develop rapport with the public; can communicate both orally and in writing; is courteous; can appraise situations; can work with the public; is able to represent group to the public; can work under pressure; is persuasive; is observant; can sell; is assertive; can advise; can make recommendations.
3. Compiles and analyzes information about potential contributors to develop mailing or contact list and to plan selling approach.	3. Is organized; can do detail work; can gather; can consolidate and summarize; can classify; does screening; can assess; collects; can expand upon; knows proper selling techniques; can plan.
4. Takes pledges or funds from contributors.	4. Collects funds; can follow through; can close the deal; can make sure information is correct; can simplify procedures; can anticipate others' needs; can meet financial goals.

(continued)

TABLE 7 (*Continued*)

Job duties	Skills required
5. Records expenses incurred and contributions received.	5. Can keep accurate records; is good with numbers; can classify numbers; is good at maintaining reports; is timely; can correctly copy information onto ledgers.
6. May organize volunteers and plan social functions to raise funds.	6. Can coordinate others; can supervise; able to direct the actions of others; can give instructions; able to coordinate fund-raising activities; able to follow through.
7. May prepare fund-raising brochures for mail solicitation.	7. Is creative; understands marketing and advertising principles; can coordinate others in department or outside companies; can brainstorm; is receptive to others' suggestions; can experiment; can work within deadlines; can get the job done.

Source for job duties: U.S. Department of Labor, Bureau of Labor Statistics, 1977, *Dictionary of Occupational Titles*.

TABLE 8
Skills for a Public Relations Specialist

Job duties	*Skills required*
1. Plans and conducts public relations program designed to create and maintain favorable public image for group.	1. Understands group's image; can develop and design program; can achieve desired results; can analyze; able to appraise situation; can critique; can evaluate; is organized; can visualize final results; is able to review; can set goals and timetables; can brainstorm; can develop policies, can make recommendations.
2. Plans and directs development and communication of information designed to keep public informed of employer's programs, accomplishments, or point of view.	2. Determines materials and/or methods to be used; implements policies; administers program; makes decisions; can get approval for ideas; conceives; supervises others; able to explain; can interpret; can inspire others to implement plan; can propose; can reshape.
3. Arranges for public relations efforts in order to meet needs, objectives, and policies of individuals, special interest groups, business concerns, nonprofit organizations, or governmental agencies, serving as volunteer.	3. Can coordinate efforts; can meet with and discuss objectives with others; prepares; prioritizes; devises strategies; schedules events or production processes; can organize; can review; can identify; can interpret.

(continued)

TABLE 8 (*Continued*)

Job duties	*Skills required*
4. Prepares and distributes fact sheets, news releases, photographs, scripts, motion pictures, or taped recordings to media representatives and other persons who may be interested in learning about or publicizing employer's activities or message.	4. Is good at detail work; is imaginative; is innovative; can type material; can gather information; makes decisions; assesses situations; has media contacts; is persuasive; is assertive; is good at following through; can communicate both orally and in writing; is good at assembling press kits; can meet deadlines; can publicize; can screen; can motivate others; can develop best strategies.
5. Purchases advertising space and time as required.	5. Analyzes best media in which to place advertisements; reviews; researches; determines best prices and exposure; makes decisions; is observant; can negotiate; can deliver copy or hire agency to do copy.

TABLE 8 (*Continued*)

Job duties	Skills required
6. Arranges for and conducts public contact programs designed to meet group's objectives, using knowledge of changing attitudes and opinions of consumers, clients, or other interest groups.	6. Develops innovative programs; able to deal with public; can assess others' attitudes; can create community feeling between group and public; can coordinate; can solve problems; is able to make presentations; can experiment; can organize; can plan; able to justify; is a risk taker; can reflect opinions; can oversee projects.
7. Promotes goodwill through such publicity efforts as speeches, exhibits, films, tours, and question/answer sessions.	7. Can be of service to others; can demonstrate sincerity; can create imaginative programs; can help people enjoy themselves or learn interesting things; can select; can improve the lot of others; can organize and coordinate events.

Source for job duties: U.S. Department of Labor, Bureau of Labor Statistics, 1977, *Dictionary of Occupational Titles.*

Why is it important for you to be in touch with your skills? First, as a woman without a college degree, you must know all of your skills. In many instances, it will be doubly hard to prove your worth to employers. This is particularly true if you want to break out of traditional low-paying jobs. In the interview, and through the use of your résumé, you must show your prospective employer that you are able to do the job. The best way is to know your skills.

Knowing your skills will build confidence and make you more

self-assured. Won't it be great to walk into a job interview knowing that you have more than 150 skills? Just imagine the confidence you will exude. Even on your old job, you will no longer think of yourself as the poor little secretary or typist, or accounting clerk or administrative assistant with few or no skills. You will walk proud, knowing that you are a person of accomplishment.

Remember, it is of course very easy to describe yourself according to your job title instead of your job duties. It's so easy to say, "I'm a secretary," when in fact you are an administrative assistant or a purchasing agent or an office manager. And it's easy to forget about skills that you have if you focus only on your job title. So look at all of your skills and propel yourself ahead!

4

Interests: Coming to Grips with What's Important

Like skills, interests can move you into new and exciting careers. We all have interests, things that we like to do. Interests can be parlayed into jobs, careers, or businesses. Many people are doing jobs that grew out of particular interests. For example, one woman loved baking pies and cakes. At first, she did it for the pleasure of her family. Then one day she made a cake for her boss. Everyone in the office loved the cake and encouraged her to bake more. She agreed and started charging $10 per cake. The local bakery soon learned of her cakes and pies, and ordered dozens every week. Soon, the woman had so much business that she was forced to quit her job. Today, she is the owner of a thriving bakery.

Another woman also loved baking. In fact, she made some of the best cookies in her town. When flea markets became popular, she carted trays of cookies to them. To her surprise, customers loved them and begged for more. Her flourishing cookie business now allows her to work part-time and devote the rest of the week to baking and selling cookies. Perhaps, one day, she'll have a Famous Amos's, David's, or Mrs. Fields' franchise business.

Still another woman has always had an interest in calligraphy. After years of experience, she developed a unique way of making cards done in calligraphy. She engaged the services of a neighbor-hood printer to make the attractive cards, and she now sells them to local specialty and card shops. Her booming business allows her to work exclusively on producing cards.

One ambitious music lover turned her interests into a part-time career. While working as a secretary, a coworker asked her to lend a collection of records for a wedding. She didn't want to lend her prized collection of music and jokingly told the coworker that she would have to come and play the records. The coworker agreed, and so began this talented woman's career as a disc jockey. She works almost every night playing music for local discos, weddings, special parties, children's parties, and so on. So she, too, has made a part-time career out of something that she loves.

Nearly everyone loves flowers. But have you ever thought of making it a career? One woman did by making beautiful flower arrangements. Soon, neighbors started asking her to make arrange-ments. She agreed and began creating special messages that were attached to the floral arrangements. People loved her special touch. A local florist was very impressed with her talents and asked her to join the staff.

Most small businesses need public relations assistance but can't afford the fees of large public relations firms. One go-getter found she was able to fill this need. She had done a great deal of public relations work for her women's group. She was always able to pack events the group gave, and her media contacts were good. One of her club members asked her to help publicize a new business. This woman did such a great job that several other businesses hired her. Now, she has many clients and is doing very well. She was able to take an interest and turn it into a marketable business.

What are your interests? Can you turn them into a new career? Don't think narrowly of careers. Think of a career as something you like to do and with which you can simultaneously make a liv-ing. Do you like writing? Maybe you can be a free-lance writer. Can you cook well? Perhaps you can start a catering business. Do you like macramé? Maybe you can make wall hangings or plant hangers. Love typing? Turn your skill into ownership of a typing service. The list is endless. Turn your interest into a career with a little ingenuity.

Table 9 shows a number of interests and the careers that can be created from them. Add your own or expand on them. Just start with your interests, and perhaps you'll find yourself working in a career that you love.

TABLE 9
Do My Interests Have Career Potential?

Interests	*Possible careers*
1. Baking, cooking, etc.	1. Catering business: selling cookies, cakes, and/or pies at flea markets, weddings, bazaars, street fairs, or other special occasions.
2. Travel	2. Arrange group trips; work for travel resorts like Club Med; social director for luxury cruise ship; flight attendant; travel agent.
3. Writing	3. Free-lance magazine writer or romance novel writer or fiction and nonfiction book writer; writer of company annual reports, etc.; writer of greeting cards; stringer for local newspaper; start a newsletter.
4. Art collecting	4. Artists' agent; give art shows to exhibit artists' work; sell art to corporations; arrange art shows for groups and organizations.
5. Flower arranging	5. Sell flower arrangements to specialty shops, individuals, and organizations. Make arrangements for special occasions like weddings or showers.

(*continued*)

TABLE 9 (*Continued*)

Interests	*Possible careers*
6. Artistic interests	6. Create paintings for individuals or organizations; create cards and postcards that feature your drawings or paintings; make posters; create T-shirts; silk-screen T-shirts; make macramé wall hangings or plant holders (start a mail-order business); make jewelry and/or belts to sell to local stores.
7. Conference planning	7. Plan conferences or meetings for women's groups, clubs, organizations, companies, or church or local political groups.
8. Calligraphy	8. Make cards, posters, or invitations for individuals and groups; start a mail-order business.
9. Music	9. Local disc jockey; music librarian for local radio station; buy, collect, and trade rare record albums, etc.; write songs or jingles; give neighborhood children and adults music lessons.
10. Public relations	10. Start a public relations firm specializing in small businesses or individuals.
11. Antiques	11. Collect antiques and sell at flea markets or street fairs; collect unusual antiques with historical value and sell to places like Sotheby's.

TABLE 9 (*Continued*)

Interests	Possible careers
12. Typing	12. Type reports, transcripts, theses, manuscripts, articles, scripts, etc.; work for lawyers, writers, students, etc.; add word processing capabilities and double your profit.
13. Matchmaking	13. Start a club for singles, seniors, or groups; organize special trips for these groups, such as "trips to nowhere," cruises, etc.
14. Shopping and other errands	14. Be a grocery or clothes shopper for those who don't have time or can't get out; specialize in gifts for those who can't shop or don't like shopping; add services like going to the cleaners or florist and other errands and build a booming business.
15. Fashion	15. Make arrangements with local wholesalers to purchase clothes in bulk; have weekly home fashion shows and sell clothes; get friends to have fashion parties (in return, give them a free dress or suit); do fashion consulting for individuals by assessing their needs and purchasing their clothing and accessories.
16. Neighborhood	16. Organize tours to historic places or other places of interest in your neighborhood; organize tours of developing neighborhoods for those who want to purchase new homes.

(*continued*)

TABLE 9 (*Continued*)

Interests	*Possible careers*
17. Social coordination	17. Organize weekly social events, such as Sunday salons that give local writers and poets a chance to read from their works (charge a fee for admission); give dances at discotheques or jazz concerts.
18. Interior decorating	18. Offer your service to new home or apartment owners who want to decorate their homes; write a decorating column for the local newspaper.
19. Organizing	19. Help individuals or small businesses organize their lives, closets, desks, file cabinets, etc.
20. Holistic health	20. Give seminars in stress management, meditation, yoga, or whatever your expertise.
21. Dance	21. Give children and adults dance lessons and have concerts; organize dance concerts for touring dance groups.

5

Plotting a New Career: The Nuts and Bolts of Career Planning

Congratulations! You have just completed five of the most difficult tasks of moving toward success: taking a good hard look at yourself, polishing your attitude, setting your goals, analyzing your skills, and determining your interests. Now it is time to put all of your feelings, responses, and knowledge of your skills and abilities together and package yourself for success.

Planning for One of the Greatest Moments in Your Life

Many people yawn when they hear about career planning. They think, "Here I go again with another boring exercise to decide what to do with my life." If you feel like this, you are limiting your success in finding a great career. It takes great career planning to land a great career. If you don't plan for your career, you'll have to take what's available. If you don't believe it, think of how you landed in your present job!

Career planning means taking control of your life. It means totally depending on yourself to get a job and career. It can be fun. It's what you make of it. So, let's make career planning an adventure.

Where do you start? Select one of two career areas that interest you. (Remember your career dreams!) Now you must get information about your selected career or careers. Where can you find this information? First, the library should have a great deal of information: books, articles, journals, and so on. Take a leisurely afternoon or Saturday and go to your public library. You will be surprised at the available information. If you don't know where to look, ask your librarian for help. Or if you live near a college or university, ask if visitors are permitted to use the career planning and placement center. Some of these centers have extensive information about careers: books, articles, special material of interest to women, and other resources.

Other great sources of career information are the professional and trade associations. Nearly every career field has a professional or trade association. Part of the mission of these groups is to acquaint prospective members of the field with career information. They will send information to you free or for a small fee. It just takes a letter to them asking for career literature, salary surveys (some organizations conduct annual salary surveys of their memberships), career bibliographies, scholarship information (some have special scholarships for women), or information about women's groups in the field. To contact professional or trade associations, ask your local librarian for *The Encyclopedia of Associations*. It is also available by writing to Gale Research Company, Book Tower, Detroit, Michigan 48226; or the National Trade and Professional Associations of the United States and Canada and Labor Unions, Garrett Park, Maryland. (See Part Two for more information on specific careers and addresses for many professional associations.)

After you receive information from a professional or trade association, pay particular attention to the education and training needed for your career, the nature of the career (what's it like?), the occupational outlook throughout the 1990s (the career's expected growth in the future, anticipated job openings, and so on), salary information (does the field offer a salary that you want?), scholarship information (does the professional or trade association offer special scholarships for women who want to pursue careers in the field? Are there special scholarships given to colleges or universities for students who want to pursue careers in the area?), and membership rosters (for names and addresses of members to contact for information about the field). You should find out if the association allows prospective members of the field to join as associate members. If so, locate a local group and attend meetings. Also ask about women's groups in the field, such as Women in Communications, and join them.

Don't forget your local bookstore. There are many career books available on various subjects. Ask the bookstore's sales staff to assist you in locating books about your field.

Matching Your Personality with the Right Industry and Company

You have selected your prospective career. Now it is time to select your new industry. There are many different industries to choose from: banking, recording, fashion, advertising, publishing, and many others. But you want to choose the right one. Why is it so important to work in the right industry? Many people think they are unhappy with their jobs; however, they are really unhappy with the industry in which they work. For example, a stylish, creative junior accountant may be happier working in the fashion industry than the banking industry. It isn't that she doesn't like accounting; it's just the wrong industry.

Do some deep soul searching, and try to determine the industry that will best suit your needs. One woman, for example, wanted to work in either the recording industry or the beauty industry. She had interests in both areas, but had to select one. She chose the field of beauty because she felt it had more financial and promotional opportunities, and that it could withstand the ups and downs of the economy better than the music industry. Today, she is working for a large cosmetics company, and has received numerous promotions.

Another woman was a word processing specialist for a corporate telecommunications company; she was miserable. As soon as she changed to the publishing industry, she was very satisfied with her job. If you are interested in word processing, sales, public relations, or legal assistance work, you are very lucky. People in these fields can choose from a wide variety of industries.

Think about it! Could you be in the right job but the wrong industry? Is there another industry where you would be happier? Is there an industry that could better utilize your skills and offer you more opportunities? If you want to totally change careers, you must also take care to select the right industry. Land in the right one, and you'll have much better job satisfaction.

Worksheet 5 will help you do some hard thinking about your future industry. First, indicate the industries that appeal to you. Next, write down the industry's image and style and determine if it matches yours. Is the industry new or old? How will this affect your getting a job and moving upward? What is the industry's growth—positive or negative?

WORKSHEET 5
Industry Selection

Industries	Does this industry appeal to me?		What is this industry's image? (aggressive, conservative)	Is this a new or old industry?	What is this industry's growth for the future?	
	Yes	No			Positive	Negative
1. Banking						
2. Recording						
3. Fashion						
4. Advertising						
5. Publishing						
6. High technology						
7. Communications						

(continued)

WORKSHEET 5 (Continued)

Industries	Does this industry appeal to me?		What is this industry's image? (aggressive, conservative)	Is this a new or old industry?	What is this industry's growth for the future?	
	Yes	No			Positive	Negative
8. Retailing						
9. Health care						
10. Manufacturing						
11. Travel						
12. Service						
13. Hotel and motel						
14. Construction						
15. Precision production						

68

16. Agricultural								
17. Legal								
18. Auto								
19. Advertising								
20. Cosmetics and beauty								
21. Magazine publishing								
22. Finance								
23. Telecommunications								
24.								

Now try to determine the best company environment for you. Every company has it own work environment. Some work environments may not suit you. Can you work where there are hundreds of cubicles lined up one next to another? Can you work in a very noisy environment? Does a time clock or sign-in sheet drive you nuts? Do you thrive in fast-paced workplaces because a too-slow work environment will lull you into boredom?

How does the company treat its employees? Are the workers treated like people or mistreated? Are employees rewarded for contributions or never acknowledged? What is the company's treatment of women and minorities? Do they hold visible and responsible positions, or are they merely window dressing? The way a company treats its employees is very revealing. Don't put yourself in a situation where you will be mistreated or prevented from moving ahead.

A good source for finding information about companies is *The 100 Best Companies to Work for in America* by Robert Levering, Milton Moskowitz, and Michael Katz (Signet, 1984).

Getting the Whole Picture: Talking to and Networking with People

Now that you have selected your future career, industry, and company, don't overlook networking in the career planning process. It is one of the most important components. Proper networking can get you a better job, more pay, and better status. Without networking you can end up with an ordinary job that is well below your abilities and skills.

In order to be an astute networker, you must be action-oriented. Since you have decided the job or career, company, and industry that you want, now take out your address book and answer these questions:

1. Is there anyone you know who works in the same or similar position?

2. Is there anyone you know who has a spouse working in the same or a similar position?

3. Is there a member of your women's or civic group or religious organization who may have friends in the position you want?

4. Does anyone you know work for your prospective company or in your new industry?

Next, ask your friends if you can look in their address books. Go over each name and ask your friends what the profession and employer of each person is. You'll probably be surprised at the wide range of people your friends know.

Now go back to the material that you received from the professional associations. Does the association's roster have members in your city? If so, contact them and ask about vital career information (skills, salary, and so forth). See if the association has local meetings in your area; these meetings are great places to network. On a very casual basis, you can ask people for information about the field, particularly job openings.

Professional associations also have annual conventions. It is here that you can learn a great deal about your field. Usually, at these conventions, speakers give workshops on various aspects of the field. This is an opportunity to learn about the field and to make contact with these speakers and/or experts in the field. You can ask for their cards and contact them at a later date. Conventions are also great places to mingle and meet people. You will be surprised at the wealth of information that you can get by having lunch or dinner with convention participants.

Don't forget local career conferences. In many cities, organizations give general career workshops for women. These workshops can be networking gold mines; they usually attract a wide spectrum of women in different career fields. Here you can meet people who can help you with your career goals. To find information about these conferences, look in your newspaper or ask your local librarian for any postings. Your career planning/placement department at a local college or university may also have this information.

Don't overlook women's magazines. Each month, most of them do profiles or articles about women in various careers or businesses. If there is an article about a woman in your prospective field, contact her for more information. Most people love to talk about themselves and their careers!

Trade magazines, available from professional and trade associations, are also a wealth of information. They also have profiles of successful people in the business. There are also general columns written by well-known authorities in the field. Contact these people and ask for information about their areas.

Remember that networking is a formal process. Like any process, you must go about it systematically. Your first important networking aid is a business card. Simply have your name, address, and phone number printed. It is easier to give people your card than to write down your number on a slip of paper that may get lost. Having cards is an inexpensive way of looking and being professional.

When you attend conferences or meetings, give out your business cards but also take them. Don't just take these cards home and dump them in a drawer. Get a business card file folder from your local stationery store and file each card.

It is also good to keep a log of the contacts made and what follow-through was done. The follow-through process is crucial. It doesn't do any good to make contacts and then lose them by not following through. Worksheet 6 is a sample networking and follow-through log. Use it!

This worksheet provides a place for the person's name, position, date and place of the first contact, and follow-through information. In the follow-through section, write the date when you contacted the person either by phone or letter. The last section is to log in the results. For example, you called Mary Williams on the 14th of May, and she couldn't talk to you, but asked you to call back in three weeks. Now, you can easily look at your log and make sure that you call her on that date. If you look at your networking and follow-through log once a day, you'll be able to keep commitments. I can't stress enough how important follow-through is.

Although most people feel comfortable talking with people they know or have met before, networking requires meeting new peo-

WORKSHEET 6
Networking and Follow-Through Log

Name	*Position and company*	*Contact date, contact place*	*Follow-through, letter or phone call*	*Results*
1.				
2.				
3.				
4.				
5.				
6.				
7.				
8.				
9.				
10.				
11.				
12.				

ple. Sometimes you will have to make "cold" calls or write letters to people you don't know. This may seem scary, but many people have been successful in this type of networking.

You may have to set up and go on fact-finding interviews. A fact-finding interview is one you set up with a person in your prospective field to ask for information about the area. Fact-finding interviews can take place with people you've met at conferences or meetings or through referrals. In the interview, you are simply asking the person:

1. How she started her career, and the various career steps

2. What skills and educational training are needed for the field

3. What the salaries are

4. What skills and abilities the person uses most on a daily basis

A fact-finding interview is not a job interview. You are not asking the person to give you a job or tell you about job openings. You are simply trying to gather information about a career area. If you approach fact-finding interviews in this manner, you will be able to get a great deal of information, and that information may ultimately lead you to a job. If you focus primarily on the person's background and training and the skills needed for a particular position, you will be able to gain access to people and ultimately gain valuable contacts.

People love to talk about themselves—keep this in mind during an interview. In the past, many of my clients and others have gone on fact-finding interviews and found that busy people will say they only have ten or fifteen minutes to spare. However, once they start talking about themselves, the interview often lasts much longer. So focus on the other person, and you'll get more information.

Since many people are frightened of approaching strangers, Figure 1 shows you how to arrange a fact-finding interview. It's a matter of getting right down to the business at hand. State your name and how you acquired the person's name and telephone number. Was it through a professional association's roster? Did you read about the person in a magazine? Was the person recommended by your family doctor?

FIGURE 1
How to Set Up a Fact-Finding Interview

RECEPTIONIST: Hello, ABC Company.

YOU: My name is Donna Jones, and I would like to speak to Ms. Karen Brown.

RECEPTIONIST: May I tell her what this is in reference to?

YOU: Yes, I received her name from _____
(professional association or person or article), and I would like to ask her a few questions.

MS. BROWN: Yes, hello, this is Karen Brown. May I help you?

YOU: Yes, Ms. Brown. My name is Donna Jones. I received your name from the_____'s member-
ship roster. I live in Chicago and am interested in learning more about the career opportunities in the area of _____ .
I understand that you have a fascinating career. I would also like to know about the skills, education and training, and salary scale for your career area. And I would like to know about the opportunities for women in the field. Would you allow me to take you to lunch to discuss these issues? Can I meet you at a convenient time and place? It would only take twenty or thirty minutes.

MS. BROWN: I'm particularly busy now. This is our rush season, but I'll be glad to go to lunch with you in a couple of weeks. Will you call me back on the fifteenth to set something up?

YOU: Thank you, Ms. Brown, for your cooperation. I will call you on the fifteenth. I really appreciate all the time that you have given me. Good-bye.

Next, tell the person exactly why you are calling. For example, if you are interested in real estate and know that the person is an authority in the field, say so! Then ask to meet the person for lunch or dinner or at a convenient place, and limit the time that you will spend. Always say, "I won't take up much of your time. It will only take fifteen or twenty minutes." This will reassure your contact that you won't be wasting time and will keep the encounter to a reasonable time. Most people will agree to this.

Of course, you will find some people who aren't agreeable. Don't let this throw you. Simply move on to your next contact. Or some people are really busy at certain times of the year and simply can't see you. If this is true, ask them for a more convenient time and get back to them. If you find that several people you've called are particularly busy, start on another part of your career planning homework and try again in a couple of days or weeks. For example, summer months may be the best times for most people. Fall is usually a busy time for everyone. Also just before major holidays like Christmas is a time when people are really busy.

The same is true about hours in the day. For example, nine and ten o'clock may be difficult times to reach people. I have found that after four o'clock is the best time to reach people. In fact, some people even answer their own phones between four and six.

Once you have reached the person and set up a time to meet, start doing your homework. You already know a great deal about your career. But write down any specific questions that you might want to ask. Table 10 gives you general questions that you can ask on fact-finding interviews.

Remember to focus on the person's move up the career ladder. People will give you many tips on getting in and moving ahead. Next, find out the skills and education needed for the job. Ask about the possibility of someone without a college degree getting a similar position. Or ask if the person knows of anyone without a degree in his or her position. If so, then ask for a referral to that person or persons. And be sure to ask for any special career advice for women who don't have college degrees.

The purpose of fact-finding interviews is to gather as much information about your prospective career as possible. To do that, you must go on several fact-finding interviews. So be prepared!

As you go on fact-finding interviews, think of yourself as a reporter who is gathering facts on a particular subject. You couldn't

TABLE 10

Questions to Ask on a Fact-Finding Interview

How did you get into the field?

How many companies have you worked for?

How did you get your present position?

What skills and educational qualifications would a person need to get an entry-level position in the field? Can a person without a college degree get hired for this job? Do you know anyone without a degree doing this type of work?

What do you do in your position? What's a typical day like?

What skills do you use in your position?

What's the next step for you on the career ladder?

Are there opportunities for women to advance in this area? What has the history been in terms of affirmative action for women?

What's the best way to get into the field?

What's the best career path to follow?

What skills does a person need for this field?

If you were hiring a person for a position in this career area, what skills and qualities would you look for?

What's the best career advice you can offer a woman like me?

---

just interview one person, because the article would be biased or slanted. You would have to talk to several people to write an objective piece. So be prepared to talk to at least five people working in your prospective career. The more people you talk to, the better your chances for success.

After you have completed your fact-finding interviews, go over all of the information that you have received. You should know a great deal about the people you've interviewed. What valuable tips did they give you? Do you now feel that you can get a job in this career area? Do you have the necessary experience and skills needed for the job?

A Word about Want Ads, Employment Agencies, and State Employment Agencies

You have now researched your career and industry and have networked with people in the field. Now you want to start looking for that coveted position. Let's say that you want to go into the cosmetics industry. You've read about the various jobs in the field and are anxious to get one. You should immediately get your Sunday newspaper and begin scanning the want-ad section. Right? Wrong! Not so fast!

As a woman without a college degree, blasting out of your present job into a new and exciting one will be more complicated. You are doing something nontraditional, and it will take a nontraditional approach to succeed.

Let's look for a moment at why using the want ads won't be the best approach for you. Take a look at some want ads. There are many job openings, but look carefully at the listed jobs' qualifications. If you want to be a secretary, the qualifications ask for typing, stenography, and other secretarial abilities. But if you are a secretary who wants to be a travel agent, the qualifications may ask for one or two years of travel agent experience. You may have some travel experience, but it is unpaid work experience. Do you think you can convince someone who placed the ad to give you special consideration? Probably not.

Usually, people who place ads in the newspaper are looking for the best candidates and can be narrow and rigid in their view of credentials. Besides, there may be a hundred other people who have worked one or two years as paid travel agents, for example, answering the ad. Why should the prospective employer listen to your story of "if given the chance, I know that I could do the job..."? He or she already has a pool of applicants with paid work experience. There's no need to take a chance on you.

Want ads have been the downfall of many a good job seeker, particularly women without college degrees. Some want ads prey on your vulnerability. You have seen them: "Fantastic job. No experience necessary. $400 a week." These ads are known as "lure ads" and are usually placed by employment agencies. These fantastic jobs really don't exist, but agencies place these ads to lure you into their offices. Once there, you'll be told that the job in the ad was just taken, but there are several secretarial jobs available. Of course, these jobs pay only $200 a week! Forget jobs that offer the world. They are usually too good to be true.

Employment agencies also place "blind" ads. These ads list a particular job with specific qualifications. Again, these jobs really don't exist. The employment agency just wants to collect résumés of certain types of workers for future reference. So, your résumé is filed away until the agency gets a call from an employer for your particular job category. In the meantime, you wait and hope for the job. Be particularly aware of ads that don't have addresses and telephone numbers. If ads only have box numbers, they may be blind ads.

If you want to break out of your present job, don't rely on employment agencies to place you in an exciting job. They are in business to get the best candidates for a particular job, but many of them are paid by the companies that have the job offering, and therefore want to best serve them. Employment agencies tend to be very conservative in viewing candidates and are careful not to damage their relationships with companies.

Another problem with many employment agencies is their view of women. Most women, even those with Ph.D.s, are often asked about secretarial skills. Just drop by an employment agency and ask them to place you in a job. If you are a woman, they will probably ask you about your typing skills. Bypass these types of agencies in your job search. You want to blast out of your present type of job, not land in a similar one.

State employment agencies attempt to find jobs for unemployed workers. Some of them do a good job of placing people but often in entry-level, low-paying positions. Most plum jobs are never posted with state employment agencies.

If you want a better job with more pay, you are going to have to take matters into your own hands. You can't afford to let someone else (employment or state employment agencies) find you a job.

You'll have to do your own muscle work, but it'll be worth it. In the time it takes you to make the rounds asking others to do your job hunting, you could be creatively landing a new job.

How do you begin? Through the exercises in this book, you will learn to become a winner at the job hunting game. You have already identified your career choice or choices and marketable skills and the industry and company where you want to work.

Now you must identify the person who can hire you. Go directly to this person and bypass the company's personnel department. As a woman without a college degree, plead your case to the person who can actually hire you. Don't plead your case to people who will screen you out of potential positions.

How do you locate the person who can hire you? Find the department where you want to work, and determine who is in charge. A simple phone call can unearth this type of information. Or there are books like *The Corporate Address Book* by Michael Levine (Putnam, 1987) that lists executives in many of the country's companies. Just locate the person in charge of hiring in your prospective department.

After you have found this person's name, telephone number, and address, contact him or her and ask about job openings in your prospective career. Once you find an opening or sympathetic ear, send the person in charge a résumé or ask for an interview.

In the next chapters, you will learn to write a résumé and cover letter that will get jobs, and you will find several surefire interviewing techniques.

6

Résumés: Dazzling Your Prospective Employer with Your Skills

Once you locate the person who can hire you, dazzle that person with your skills. You will do this through your résumé.

If written correctly, a résumé can be a job seeker's best job-seeking tool. If done incorrectly, it can be your worst enemy. Résumés can open or shut doors. Learn to write one correctly, and you'll develop a lifelong skill.

A résumé is a brief synopsis of your educational and work history. It isn't an autobiography or document that lists everything you've done in your life. A résumé is your "sixty-second commercial." And as in any commercial, you should only use relevant, marketable material.

A résumé shouldn't be written for your own pleasure. It should be written with your prospective employer in mind. After all, she or he is hiring you. Shouldn't you gear your résumé to reflect what she or he needs in a future employee? Although this is good common sense, many people write their résumés from their own point of view and wonder why they don't get jobs.

This is not necessarily the fault of the job seeker. After all, no one really taught you how to write a résumé. As a high school graduate, you were probably never officially introduced to résumé writing. High school personnel probably assumed that you would learn résumé writing in college. Since you may have graduated from high school and started working in entry-level positions, you were probably required to only complete applications. There wasn't a need for a résumé.

Now things have changed. You really want a better-paying job. You want to blast out of the typical jobs for women without college degrees. You can do the job, but you must show your prospective employer. Put it in your résumé.

How do you begin? Like everything else, résumés take preparation. You must begin to look at two very important things: you and the job you want. First, let's look at you! What relevant things concerning *you* will be put in the résumé? To assess this, you must begin by taking a look at all of your educational and work history.

Let's look at Worksheet 7. This chart will help you discover many things about yourself. It is the foundation from which you will build your résumé. It is called Remembering: Preliminary Résumé Analysis because we often forget so many relevant things about our past. In fact, one of these forgotten facts may be crucial to your getting a job one day.

WORKSHEET 7
Remembering: Preliminary
Résumé Analysis

HIGH SCHOOL EDUCATION

1. Where did you go to high school? (Write down name, city, state; if you received a general equivalency diploma (GED) skip questions 3 to 9.)

---

2. What courses did you take? (Write down as many as you can remember.)

_____

_____

_____

_____

_____

_____

_____

_____

3. What type of high school diploma did you receive (academic or commercial)?

_____

_____

4. Which were your best courses in high school?

_____

_____

5. Why?_____

_____

6. Which courses were your worst?

_____

_____

7. Why? _____

_____

8. Did you win any awards, honors, or contests in high school?

_____

_____

9. What were your extracurricular activities (president of a club, member of a club, and so on)?

_____

_____

COLLEGE

Name all of the institutions where you went, regardless of whether or not you completed your course work and even if it was a long time ago. (If you didn't go to college, skip to the next section.)

Institution #1

Name _____ City _____ State _____

1. What years did you attend? _____

2. What courses did you take? What were your grades in each course?

_____

_____

_____

_____

_____

_____

_____

_____

_____

3. Which courses did you like best? Why?

_____

_____

4. Which courses did you like least? Why?

_____

_____

5. What was your major? What was your minor?

_____

6. What were your extracurricular activities? (Officer of a club? Member of a club? Member of a sports team?)

_____

_____

7. What were your honors or awards?

_____

_____

8. What were the total number of credits that you received at this institution?

_____

Institution #2
Name _____ City _____ State _____

1. What years did you attend? _____

2. What courses did you take? What were your grades in each course?

_____

_____

_____

_____

_____

_____

_____

_____

_____

3. Which courses did you like best? Why?

_____

_____

4. Which courses did you like least? Why?

_____

_____

5. What was your major? What was your minor?

_____

6. What were your extracurricular activities? (Officer of a club? Member of a club? Member of a sports team?)

_____

_____

7. What were your honors or awards?

_____

_____

8. What were the total number of credits that you received at this institution?

_____

Institution #3
Name _____ City _____ State _____

1. What years did you attend? _____

2. What courses did you take? What were your grades in each course?

_____

_____

_____

_____

_____

_____

_____

_____

_____

3. Which courses did you like best? Why?

_____

_____

4. Which courses did you like least? Why?

_____

_____

5. What was your major? What was your minor?

_____

6. What were your extracurricular activities? (Officer of a club? Member of a club? Member of a sports team?)

_____

_____

7. What were your honors or awards?

_____

_____

8. What were the total number of credits that you received at this institution?

_____

BUSINESS OR VOCATIONAL SCHOOL

Institution #1
Name _____ City _____ State _____

1. What years did you attend? _____

2. What courses did you take? What were your grades in each course?

_____

_____

_____

_____

_____

_____

_____

_____

_____

_____

3. Which courses did you like best? Why?

_____

_____

4. Which courses did you like least? Why?

_____

_____

5. What skills did you receive as a result of your training, for example, typing, shorthand, or computer operation? What are the levels of your skills; for example, can you type 50 WPM?

_____

_____

6. Did you receive a diploma or certificate? What kind and what year?

_____

_____

Institution #2
Name _____ City _____ State _____

1. What years or months did you attend there? _____

2. Which courses did you take? How well did you do in each course?

_____

_____

_____

_____

_____

_____

_____

_____

_____

3. Which courses did you like best? Why?

_____

_____

4. Which courses did you like least? Why?

_____

_____

5. What skills did you receive as a result of your training? What are the levels of your skills?

_____

_____

6. Did you receive a diploma or certificate? What kind and what year?

_____

Institution #3
Name _____ City _____ State _____

1. What years or months did you attend there? _____

2. Which courses did you take? How well did you do in each course?

_____

_____

_____

_____

_____

_____

_____

_____

3. Which courses did you like best? Why? _____

_____

4. Which courses did you like least? Why? _____

_____

5. What skills did you receive as a result of your training? What are the levels of your skills?

_____

_____

6. Did you receive a diploma or certificate? What kind and what year?

_____

WORK EXPERIENCE

Job #1

1. What was the title of your first job after high school?

_____

2. What was the name and address of your employer?

_____

_____

3. What years were you employed? _____

4. What skills did you learn as a result of doing this job? (Think of your job duties instead of your job title.)

Job duties	These duties translate to the following skills

5. What are five things you did at this job that make you feel proud (such as, developed a filing system that improved efficiency)?

a. _____

_____

b. _____

_____

c. _____

_____

d. _____

_____

e. _____

_____

Job #2

1. What was the title of your second job after high school?

_____

2. What was the name and address of your employer?

_____

_____

3. What years were you employed? _____

4. What skills did you learn as a result of doing this job? (Think of your job duties instead of your job title.)

Job duties	These duties translate to the following skills

5. What are five things you did at this job that make you feel proud?

a. _____

_____

b. _____

_____

c. _____

_____

d. _____

_____

e. _____

_____

Job #3

1. What was the title of your third job after high school?

_____

2. What was the name and address of your employer?

_____

3. What years were you employed? _____

4. What skills did you learn as a result of doing this job? (Think of your job duties instead of your job title.)

Job duties	These duties translate to the following skills

5. What are five things you did at this job that make you feel proud?

a. _____

_____

b. _____

_____

c. _____

_____

d. _____

_____

e. _____

_____

Job #4

1. What was the title of your fourth job after high school?

   _____

2. What was the name and address of your employer?

   _____

   _____

3. What years were you employed? _____

4. What skills did you learn as a result of doing this job? (Think of your job duties instead of your job title.)

Job duties	These duties translate to the following skills

5. What are five things you did at this job that make you feel proud?

   a. _____

   _____

   b. _____

   _____

   c. _____

d. _____

_____

e. _____

_____

Job #5

1. What was the title of your fifth professional job?

_____

2. What was the name and address of your employer?

_____

_____

3. What years were you employed? _____

4. What skills did you learn as a result of doing this job? (Think of your job duties instead of your job title.)

Job duties	*These duties translate to the following skills*

5. What are five things you did at this job that make you feel proud?

a. _____

_____

b. _____

_____

c. _____

_____

d. _____

_____

e. _____

_____

UNPAID WORK EXPERIENCE

1. List all of the unpaid work experiences that you have had (dates, titles, and skills). For example, this could be volunteer, civic, religious, or women's group work.

Name of group	Years with group	Offices held, years	Skills learned
1.			
2.			
3.			
4.			
5.			

Name of group	Years with group	Offices held, years	Skills learned
6.			
7.			
8.			
9.			
10.			

2. List five achievements from your unpaid work experience.

   a. _____

   b. _____

   c. _____

   d. _____

   e. _____

3. Did you receive any awards, honors, or plaques for your unpaid work? From whom? When?

   _____

   _____

   _____

   _____

   _____

4. What clubs or organizations are you in currently? If you hold office in any group, what office and for how long have you held it?

_____

_____

_____

_____

_____

5. Have you traveled extensively? If so, in what countries or states?

_____

_____

_____

_____

The first section of the worksheet deals with your education. Let's look at Question 1. Put down the name, city, and state of your high school. In Question 2, you are asked to list your high school courses. Sharpen your memory and put down as many as possible. If you have forgotten, send a letter to your high school and get a copy of your records. Although many of you may think this is irrelevant, it is an integral part of your résumé planning. Remembering your high school courses will help you determine many of your likes, dislikes, strengths, and weaknesses. As time passes, we all forget vital aspects of our lives.

Question 3 asks what type of diploma you received. This will help you understand the whys behind the courses you took. Were you in an academic or commercial program? Did your high school courses prepare you for certain careers?

Questions 4 and 5 ask what were your best courses in high school and why you liked them. Again, you are trying to determine your likes and dislikes and interests. Questions 6 and 7 will help you determine those courses that you didn't like and why. These four questions will also help you understand yourself a little better.

Question 8 will help you uncover some forgotten skills. For example, did you win the tenth grade public speaking contest? Why is this important? You may now, for example, feel that you could never speak in public. But remember back to the day when you won that contest. Think of how confident and brave you were. Remember the applause! Think about the judges' reactions to your speech and your own reaction to receiving the prize. Perhaps you can do it again. With a little brushing up, you can speak in front of large groups again. Skills are rarely lost. Often, you may only need to get in touch with a forgotten skill and brush up on it.

Question 9 asks what your extracurricular activities were. Were you president of a club in high school? If so, it shows that you had leadership ability. If you were once a leader, you can still be one. Or were you a member of a girls' sports team? That means that you were a team player.

Many women without college degrees have had some college. Yet it is surprising that many ignore this on their résumés. They may feel ashamed because they didn't finish their course work. Some may feel their course work was so long ago that it isn't relevant. This isn't true! Regardless of when you went to college, your course work still counts. Even if you only have a few credits, you did attend college and were successful in those courses. Perhaps you even took a course that may be relevant to a position that you want. This is why it is so important to remember all aspects of your educational training. And if you are in an interview, never lose a job because you can't remember one important course or factor of your training.

The college section of Worksheet 7 explores your educational work at the college or colleges you attended. If you can't remember years and courses, send for your transcript. Colleges keep records of all their former students. What was the name of the college you attended and the city and state where it is located? Now, list the courses and grades that you received in these courses. The courses will help you remember any course work relevant to your future career. The grades will let you know how proficient you were in those subjects. Your best-liked and least-liked courses will tell you something about your interests and skills.

Your extracurricular activities will tell you what kind of student you were. Were you an egghead type, who didn't join in any activities? Or were you active in clubs? Having been a club officer, for example, indicates that you have leadership qualities. Participating in extracurricular activities means you were a well-rounded student.

What honors and awards did you receive? Were you on the Dean's list or inducted into a special honor society for your major area?

What was your major? Majors indicate your main area of interest. Did you take major courses that will help you in your new career? What was your minor, or was there a special area other than your major in which you took many courses?

What are the total number of credits that you received at your college? Many people leave this vital fact off their résumés. If you have a half year or one, two, or three years of college, this is important. Again, don't disregard it because you didn't get a degree.

Look at the next section, marked Business or Vocational School. Did you receive specialized training at one of these schools? Many women who don't have college degrees have attended business, vocational, or trade schools or have taken special certificate courses through their unions or at colleges or night high schools. Be sure to write down the years that you attended. This information will go on your résumé. What courses did you take, how well did you do in them, and which ones did you like best or least? This should be very revealing. For example, you may think that you like or have strengths in things that you really don't.

What skills did you learn from your specialized training? Did you learn to type 50 words per minute (WPM) or do shorthand at 80 WPM? Did you learn math or writing skills? Did you have computer training? Or did you take a course in office procedures?

Be sure to indicate any diploma or certificate you received for this training and the year you received it.

The section marked Work Experience deals with your post–high school work experience. Although you may not use all of these jobs on your résumé (just the relevant ones), be sure to be as complete as possible. If you have had more jobs than there is space to record them, list them on a separate page, using the same format.

For your first professional job, list your job title, your employer, and your employer's city and state. Next, list the years of employment. As you did in the chapter on skills for your present job, list the job duties of your first job after high school. Next to it, use the skills list and try to determine the skills that these duties translate to.

Why should you do this? Too often, job seekers only casually list a few job functions for their first professional positions. But employers want to know your true work level and responsibilities and the progressive level of responsibility that you have had.

Now, look at your achievements on the job. What things did you do to help the company? What things are you the most proud of? For example, did you develop a filing system that increased office efficiency by 50 percent? This information should go on your résumé. A prospective employer wants to know not only that you were a file clerk but also what results were accomplished. Since résumés should be results-oriented, or list the results of your work, try to remember some of your accomplishments on the job. Think about the wonderful things you did for the office that no one appreciated or patted you on the back for. This is a great way to discover your job-related accomplishments.

The last section focuses on your unpaid work experience. Many women who don't have college degrees have gained invaluable experience through religious, civic, or women's group work. Some have raised thousands of dollars for a cause. Others have promoted and publicized events and made them successful. Still others have held offices and kept organizations functioning properly. Yet many of you don't think of these positions as ones where you gained a great many skills. Like Carolyn in Chapter 1, you don't cherish the skills gained from these experiences because you weren't paid for the work.

In this society, we are taught to disregard or think less of things that don't have monetary attachments. But if you know how to raise funds or do public relations, it doesn't matter that you learned those skills in unpaid work. These skills belong to you, and no one can take them away. (Look back at the skills lists in Tables 7 and 8 to help you remember any fund-raising or public relations skills.)

Think of five achievements from your unpaid experience. For example, if you are a member of a ladies auxiliary group, what have you contributed to the organization? Did you sit on a committee that gave a benefit to raise scholarship money for neighborhood children? What was your contribution to the committee and the fund-raising program?

Did you receive any awards, honors, or plaques for your unpaid work? You may have received numerous awards for volunteer work, but again, do not devalue them because they are associated with unpaid work experience. Some of your awards are probably quite impressive, and you should put them down.

List all of the groups that you presently are a member of. Give particular importance to any professional groups, such as The National Association of Secretaries. Put down the years and offices held in these groups.

Finally, if you have traveled extensively throughout Europe, Africa, Asia, the Caribbean, or Central or South America, list the countries where you have traveled. If you have traveled extensively throughout the United States, for example, name the states. Many employers want to know that prospective employees have traveled. An extensive traveler may be viewed as someone who knows countries and their customs. Or you may be viewed as someone who has travel savvy and who will be a welcomed member of a company where extensive travel is required of employees.

Choose the Best Type of Résumé for You

Since you have done such a great job of analyzing yourself, it is now time to do your résumé. But before you can write one you must know the different types of résumés, the dos and don'ts, and how to technically lay a résumé out.

There are three types of résumés. The most familiar and most talked about in many résumé books is the chronological type. It is the résumé that most job seekers use. But there are other types: the functional and the combination résumés. You will learn which is best for you.

What is the chronological résumé? It lists your present and former work and educational experience in reverse chronological order. It is best used for people who have had a steady work background (no gaps) and want to move up to a similar or more advanced position in their same line of work.

In the chronological résumé, you list either your educational or your work history first. Since you have probably been working for some time and your work history is probably most relevant and strongest, list your work experience first.

Figure 2 shows a typical chronological résumé. Mary Louis is a secretary, and her résumé reflects steady employment in the field. This résumé is used because Mary wants to remain a secretary but change to a better-paying job. As we see, she lists her work experience first. At the top, she lists her present job, then her last job, and so on. Next, she lists her educational experience in the same reverse chronological order.

FIGURE 2
Chronological Résumé

Mary Louis
441 Chase Street
Detroit, Michigan 99066
(608) 339-9807

WORK EXPERIENCE:

1980–Present	Wakeren Brothers, Detroit, Michigan.
	Secretary
	Type correspondence and other documents. Report to three administrators. Take shorthand. Handle travel itinerary for bosses. Responsible for setting up meetings for supervisors.
1978–1980	Talmier Inc., Lathrop Village, Michigan.
	Secretary
	Typed correspondence for boss.

(continued)

Composed letters. Typed reports.
Scheduled appointments for boss.
Answered telephones.

EDUCATION:

1977–1978   TCU Business Academy, Detroit,
                             Michigan. Received certificate in
                             secretarial studies.

1974–1977   Wilson High School, Detroit, Michigan.
                             Received high school diploma.

SPECIAL SKILLS:

Can type 50 WPM; can take shorthand at 60 WPM; have knowledge of
office machines including duplicating and adding machines.

REFERENCES:

Furnished upon request.

The functional résumé is best for people who want to change careers or for those with on-again, off-again employment. It highlights skill areas and gives you more control over which skills you want highlighted. It gives you a perfect opportunity to put yourself in the place of the employer and decide what he or she is looking for.

Figure 3 shows a functional résumé for Mary Louis. She now selects the functional résumé because she wants to change careers and become a travel agent. Since her work employment has primarily been secretarial, she now wants to emphasize her traveling experience and expertise and skills that will relate to a travel agent's position. She has some of a travel agent's skills but must put those in résumé form.

FIGURE 3
Functional Résumé

Mary Louis
441 Chase Street
Detroit, Michigan 99066
(608) 339-9807

MAJOR SKILLS AREAS:

TRAVEL

Responsible for planning travel itineraries for three departmental managers. Arrange accommodations and other travel services for executives traveling to Rome, Paris, London, Stockholm, Madrid, Toronto, Cairo, Hong Kong, etc. Confer with executives to determine preferences in mode of transportation, travel dates, and accommodations. Send for, receive, and distribute travel brochures and publications on various countries to executives.

In charge of computing travel and accommodation costs to keep within budget. Book executives on appropriate transportation carrier and make hotel reservations. Obtain and distribute tickets.

Designed tour package for Wakeren Brothers conference in Los Angeles. Directly negotiated with transportation carrier and hotels. Made all travel and hotel arrangements. Was able to get specials like hospitality suites, restaurants, and hotel-shop discounts and complimentary airline tickets for some of the participants. Made all conference meeting-rooms arrangements. Calculated costs of conference per person to keep within travel budget.

Conceived of, developed, and organized group travel for a group of 100 adults and children to Nassau, Bahama Islands. Under the auspices of the Lathrop Village Volunteers of the Community, arranged trip for group. Determined best and most cost-effective group package by canvassing different airlines, hotels, and the tourist board. Negotiated with a major hotel in Nassau and arranged for group accommodations. Developed local sight-seeing tour of Nassau for participants. Arranged for special discounts in stores, casino, and restaurants. Designed "coupon booklet" for participants. Also developed group tour to Disney World in 1979; to Miami in 1980.

(continued)

Have knowledge of three languages: Spanish, French, and Italian. Have traveled extensively to London; Dublin; Paris; Honolulu; Ontario and Toronto; Kingston and Montego Bay, Jamaica, West Indies; San Juan, Puerto Rico; Nassau, Bahama Islands; St. Thomas, Virgin Islands; Rome; Casablanca; and New Delhi. Have also traveled to thirty U.S. cities including New York; Minneapolis; San Francisco; Los Angeles; Chicago; Washington, D.C.; Miami; Richmond and Virginia Beach, Virginia; and Hilton Head, South Carolina.

Have lived in six countries including France, Spain, Italy, England, and India.

SPECIAL SKILLS:

Typing 50 WPM; shorthand 60 WPM; have knowledge of calculator, adding machine, and duplicating machine.

EDUCATION:

1977–1978   TCU Business Academy, Detroit, Michigan. Received certificate in secretarial studies.

1974–1977   Wilson High School, Detroit, Michigan. Received high school diploma.

SPECIAL TRAINING:

American Society of Travel Agents, Washington, D.C. Received certificate for home study course.

REFERENCES:

Furnished upon request.

Mary has learned what skills are required for travel agents. They must plan itineraries and arrange accommodations and other travel services for customers of travel agencies; converse with customers to determine destination, mode of transportation, travel dates, financial considerations, and accommodations required; plan or describe and sell itinerary package tours; give customers brochures and publications concerning travel and containing information such as local customs, points of interest, and special events occurring in various locations, or foreign-country regulations such as consular requirements, rates of monetary exchange, and currency limitations; and quote costs of package tours or compute cost of travel and accommodations using calculator and/or adding machine, tariff books, and hotel rate books. An agent also books customers on transportation carriers and makes hotel reservations using telephone or typewriter; writes or obtains travel tickets for transportation or tour and collects payment; may specialize in foreign or domestic service, individual or group travel, specific geographical areas, airplane charters, or package tours by bus.

Mary now tries to identify her skills that will translate to travel. For example, she regularly makes travel arrangements for her bosses and other executives in the company. In fact, she is considered the unofficial travel agent for these executives. Once, she set up the travel arrangements for all the members of her department to attend a company conference.

Mary was also instrumental in developing a tour package for a group, the Lathrop Village Volunteers of the Community. In 1978, she put together a group tour for the Lathrop Village Volunteers to Nassau, in the Bahama Islands, in which 100 parents and children participated. She includes this on her résumé because through this project she gained a great deal of insight into the travel business. She figures that the valuable skills gained from the experience can be transferred to a paid job. She also arranged other group tours, including one for the Lathrop Village Volunteers to Disney World in 1979 and to Miami in 1980.

Mary knows three languages—Spanish, French, and Italian—fluently. Since knowledge of different languages is important for travel agents specializing in foreign travel, she highlights this. She has also traveled extensively to England, Ireland, France, Canada, Morocco, and India. Because of her traveling, she has some knowledge of the countries, the people, and the customs, which are important assets for a travel agent. She has also probably stayed in hotels in these countries and has intimate knowledge of these accommodations. This information can be helpful to her future clients.

While married, Mary lived in six countries: Spain, India, England, France, Italy, and Germany. Her intimate knowledge of these countries, the people, and the customs will make her a valuable travel agent.

Because typing and shorthand can be helpful to any travel agent, Mary includes these types of skills under the section Special Skills. She also includes her knowledge of using a calculator, adding machine, and duplicating machine, which are tools a travel agent needs.

If Mary had used the chronological résumé, emphasizing her travel experience would have been more difficult. The functional résumé is best in her case because it emphasizes her travel experience and deemphasizes the secretarial work. It also gives her an opportunity to highlight related community and volunteer work.

Figure 4 shows the combination résumé. It is a combination of the chronological and functional résumés. Many people prefer this type of résumé, because it combines the best of the two other types: it emphasizes traditional aspects of the chronological résumé and also highlights skills from the functional résumé. Since many employers are most familiar with the chronological résumé and may want to see employers and dates, the combination résumé offers them both.

FIGURE 4
Combination Résumé

Mary Louis
441 Chase Street
Detroit, Michigan 99066
(608) 339-9807

MAJOR SKILLS AREAS:

TRAVEL

Responsible for planning travel itineraries for three departmental managers. Arrange accommodations and other travel services for executives traveling to Rome, Paris, London, Stockholm, Madrid, Toronto, Cairo,

Hong Kong, etc. Confer with executives to determine preferences in mode of transportation, travel dates, and accommodations. Send for, receive, and distribute travel brochures and publications on various countries to executives.

In charge of computing travel and accommodation costs to keep within budget. Book executives on appropriate transportation carrier and make hotel reservations. Obtain and distribute tickets.

Designed tour package for Wakeren Brothers conference in Los Angeles. Directly negotiated with transportation carrier and hotels. Made all travel and hotel arrangements. Was able to get specials like hospitality suites, restaurants, and hotel-shop discounts, and complimentary airline tickets for some of the participants. Made all conference meeting-rooms arrangements. Calculated costs of conference per person to keep within travel budget.

Conceived of, developed, and organized group travel for a group of 100 adults and children to Nassau, Bahama Islands. Under the auspices of the Lathrop Village Volunteers of the Community, arranged trip for group. Determined best and most cost-effective group package by canvassing different airlines, hotels, and the tourist board. Negotiated with a major hotel in Nassau and arranged for group accommodations. Developed local sight-seeing tour of Nassau for participants. Arranged for special discounts in stores, casino, and restaurants. Designed "coupon booklet" for participants. Also developed tour group to Disney World in 1979; to Miami in 1980.

Have knowledge of three languages: Spanish, French, and Italian. Have traveled extensively to London; Dublin; Paris; Honolulu; Ontario and Toronto; Kingston and Montego Bay, Jamaica, West Indies; San Juan, Puerto Rico; Nassau, Bahama Islands; St. Thomas, Virgin Islands; Rome; Casablanca; and New Delhi. Have also traveled to thirty U.S. cities including New York; Minneapolis; San Francisco; Los Angeles; Chicago; Washington, D.C.; Miami; Richmond and Virginia Beach, Virginia; and Hilton Head, South Carolina.

Have lived in six countries including France, Spain, Italy, England, and India.

(continued)

MAJOR EMPLOYMENT:

1980–Present	Wakeren Brothers, Detroit, Michigan.
	Secretary
1978–1980	Talmier Inc., Lathrop Village, Michigan.
	Secretary

EDUCATION:

1977–1978	TCU Business Academy, Detroit, Michigan. Received certificate in secretarial studies.
1974–1977	Wilson High School, Detroit, Michigan. Received high school diploma.

SPECIAL TRAINING:

American Society of Travel Agents, Washington, D.C. Received certificate for home study course.

SPECIAL SKILLS:

Typing 50 WPM; shorthand 60 WPM; have knowledge of calculator, adding machine, and duplicating machine.

REFERENCES:

Furnished upon request.

In Mary's combination résumé, she simply adds her dates of employment and employers.

Putting the Résumé Together

Now that you've seen Mary's three types of résumés, let's begin step-by-step to put together your résumé. Today, you will get out of the habit of writing one résumé for several jobs that you want. You will prepare a résumé for each job that you want. Each one will be tailor-made to the position you are pursuing. You must determine what each employer is looking for and put yourself in the place of the employer. You are going to show each prospective employer, in your résumé, that you are tailor-made for the position. So you must know what each job requires in terms of skills.

First, put your name, full address, and work and home telephone numbers at the top of your résumé. It is very important to put your business number or one where you can be reached during the day. If a prospective employer wants to get in touch with you, it will probably be during business hours. But if you don't want your present employer to know that you are looking for a job, use a number where messages can be left. Either use an answering service or a reliable message taker. Many jobs have been lost simply because the employer couldn't get in touch with the job seeker.

First, you will learn to write the chronological résumé, using Figure 5 as a guide. If you have had a steady work history and want to move to a better job in the same field, this is the résumé for you.

FIGURE 5
Skeleton Chronological Résumé

Name
Address
Phone Numbers (Home and Office)

MAJOR EMPLOYMENT:

1981–Present   United Life Insurance Company, Miami, Florida.

Insurance Agent

Sold $800,000 in Life insurance to 20 clients. Developed sales system that helped clients better understand types of policies and coverage and the benefit of getting extended coverage. This method increased sales by 50 percent, and so on.

_____

_____

_____

_____

_____

_____

Dates: Company_____

City_____ State_____

Job Titles_____

_____

Job Duties_____

_____

Dates: Company_____

                                City_____ State_____

                                Job Titles_____

                                _____

                                Job Duties_____

                                _____

EDUCATION:

1979–1980   Royce Business School, Miami, Florida.
                                Received certificate in secretarial studies.

1975–1978   Lellwood High School, Miami, Florida.
                                Received high school diploma
                                (commercial studies)

PROFESSIONAL ASSOCIATIONS:

1981–Present   Member of the Professional Secretaries
                                Association International (Miami Chapter)

REFERENCES:

Furnished upon request.

Write down your work experience. On the left-hand side, put your employment dates. It isn't necessary to put the full date, such as September 30, 1980, to December 1, 1982. You can simply put September 1980–December 1982.

On the right side, put your present employer and employment address, using only the city and state. Don't use full addresses. Underneath, put your job title. Now, begin the description of your job duties. Use crisp action words such as those listed in Figure 6. And don't forget to use the present verb tense in describing the duties of your present position.

FIGURE 6
Résumé Action Words

Accomplish	Conduct	Draft
Activate	Construct	Draw
Adapt	Consult	Edit
Address	Contact	Educate
Adjust	Contribute	Encourage
Administer	Control	Enforce
Advertise	Cook	Enlarge
Advocate	Cooperate	Enlist
Allocate	Coordinate	Entertain
Analyze	Copy	Establish
Anticipate	Counsel	Estimate
Approve	Count	Evaluate
Arrange	Create	Examine
Assemble	Critique	Exercise
Assign	Dance	Exhibit
Audit	Debate	Expand
Balance	Decide	Expedite
Bargain	Decorate	Experiment
Brainstorm	Define	Explain
Budget	Delegate	Explore
Build	Deliver	Facilitate
Calculate	Demonstrate	Feed
Care for	Design	File
Catalog	Detail	Find
Cater	Detect	Fix
Change	Determine	Follow through
Classify	Develop	Forecast
Coach	Devise	Formulate
Collaborate	Diagnose	Gather
Collect	Direct	Govern
Combine	Discipline	Graph
Communicate	Discover	Guide
Compare	Discuss	Handle
Compile	Dispense	Help
Compose	Display	Identify
Compute	Distribute	Imagine
Conceive	Do bookkeeping	Implement

Improve
Initiate
Index
Innovate
Inspect
Instruct
Interview
Invent
Investigate
Judge
Justify
Lead
Lecture
Lobby
Locate
Maintain
Make
Manage
Manipulate
Map
Measure
Mediate
Meet the public
Moderate
Modify
Monitor
Navigate
Nurse
Obtain
Operate
Order
Organize
Oversee

Paint
Perform
Persuade
Plan
Politick
Predict
Prepare
Preside
Print
Prioritize
Process
Produce
Program
Promote
Proofread
Protect
Purchase
Raise funds
Read
Recognize
Recommend
Reconcile
Record
Recruit
Rectify
Reduce
Rehabilitate
Reorganize
Report
Represent
Reproduce
Research
Resolve

Restore
Review
Rewrite
Scan
Schedule
Screen
Simplify
Sing
Solve
Speak
Stimulate
Strategize
Strengthen
Summarize
Supervise
Systemize
Take risks
Talk
Target
Teach
Think
Train
Transmit
Treat
Troubleshoot
Type
Update
Use instruments
Utilize
Validate
Visualize
Work with others
Work with precision
Write

Your résumé should be results-oriented. It's great to say, for example, you were in charge of the office. But what was the result? Isn't it more effective to say that you designed a new office system that increased efficiency by 70 percent? Go back to Worksheet 7 and review your answers to the question regarding the five things you did at each of your professional jobs that made you feel proud. What were those accomplishments, what were the results?

Since your résumé will be oriented toward the position that you want, go back to the career material from the professional associations or your fact-finding interview notes. Determine which skills are needed for the position you want. Or read the U.S. Department of Labor's *Dictionary of Occupational Titles* (DOT), which lists skills for hundreds of jobs. You can get this book at your local library or by writing to the Superintendent of Documents, U.S. Government Printing Office, Washington, D.C. 20402.

The DOT lists, for example, the skills of an insurance agent:

> Sells insurance to new and present clients, recommending amount and type of coverage based on analysis of prospect's circumstances. Compiles lists of prospective clients to provide leads for additional business. Contacts prospects and explains features and merits of policies offered, utilizing persuasive sales techniques. Calculates and quotes premium rates for recommended policies, using adding machine and rate books. Calls on policy-holders to deliver and explain policy, to suggest additions or changes in insurance program, or to make changes in beneficiaries. May collect weekly or monthly premiums from policy-holders and keep record of payments. Must have license issued by state. May work independently, selling a variety of insurance such as life, fire and casualty, and marine.

You can see that the DOT can be very helpful in determining skills needed for your present position. This book is also helpful in writing a functional or combination résumé.

With the functional and combination résumés, the DOT can help you determine major skill areas needed for your new job. For example, if you want to go into public relations, you may determine that the major skill areas are public relations and writing.

Avoiding Mistakes: "Before" and "After" Résumés

One of the best ways to learn how to write an effective résumé is to look at the mistakes of others. In Figures 7 through 18 are examples of "before" and "after" résumés. All of these women are high school graduates and have typical jobs for women without college degrees. They attempted to write their own résumés and made very common, understandable mistakes.

Let's look at Figure 7. Deloris Stuart's job title is Secretary III, but she has actually performed many job duties of an administrative assistant. She wants to move up to an administrative assistant's or word processing manager's position.

Like the typical résumé writer, Deloris doesn't fully explain all of her duties. As a result, her "before" résumé identifies her as a secretary instead of an administrative assistant. Since she wants an administrative assistant's position, she is doing herself a disservice by short-selling her administrative skills. And although she supervises workers now and has in the past, she doesn't highlight her supervisory skills.

FIGURE 7
Stress Duties and Skills: "Before" Résumé

Deloris Stuart
916 Main Street
Marietta, Illinois 80097
Home Phone (618) 896-6743
Office Phone (618) 355-9090

OBJECTIVE:

Challenging administrative assistant position

WORK EXPERIENCE:

1983–Present	Lincoln Textile, Marietta, Illinois.
	Secretary III
	Compose and type correspondence for executive vice president. Supervise staff of ten clerical workers. Responsible for overall office management. In charge of simplification of reporting procedures and suggestions systems. Responsible for increasing office production. Responsible for the collection and preparation of all operating reports. In charge of reviewing all new hires, transfers, and terminations of staff.
1980–1983	Wilson Mills, Marietta, Illinois.
	Word Processing Supervisor
	Supervised twelve word processing specialists in a word processing department. Responsible for the production of correspondence, reports, and documents for 20 managers. Responsible for training staff members.

1971–1980	Secretary
	Handled secretarial duties for vice president in charge of marketing. Scheduled trips and handled itineraries for boss. Learned IBM word processing in company training program and promoted to word processing supervisor in 1980.

EDUCATION:

1983	UPT Business Academy, Marietta, Illinois. Currently working toward associate degree in secretarial science with specialty in word processing. Have 40 credits in courses such as administrative assistant I and II and fundamentals of word processing.
1980	Allstate Business School, Marietta, Illinois. Completed certificate program in word processing.
1971–1973	Allstate Business School, Marietta, Illinois. Received certificate in secretarial studies.
1968–1971	Marietta High School, Marietta, Illinois. Received high school diploma.

SPECIAL SKILLS:

Typing (80 WPM), Gregg shorthand (80 WPM), knowledge of IBM word processing system (PC) and IBM Memorywriter; knowledge of duplicating machines, calculators, and adding machines.

REFERENCES:

Furnished upon request.

In Deloris's "after" résumé (Figure 8), she uses the functional type to camouflage her present job title, Secretary III, and focuses on administrative and word processing supervision skills. In this way, she can best explain her administrative duties.

FIGURE 8
Stress Duties and Skills: "After" Résumé

Deloris Stuart
916 Main Street
Marietta, Illinois 80097
Home Phone (618) 896-6743
Office (618) 355-9090

MAJOR SKILLS AREAS:

ADMINISTRATIVE

Responsible for coordinating office services such as personnel. Study management methods in order to improve work flow. Develop strategies to simplify reporting procedures. Designed office layout. Developed suggestions system that increased staff morale and output by 50 percent. Created new work management system that increased efficiency of office production. Devised new record-keeping system that eliminated errors.

Coordinate the collection and preparation of all operating reports (time and attendance records, new hires, transfers, and terminations of clerical and secretarial staff) and budget expenditures and statistical records of performance data. In charge of preparing reports including conclusions and recommendations for solution of administrative problems. Recommended purchase of and did cost analysis for new office equipment that has substantially saved company money. Researched, developed, and recommended purchase of new telecommunications system that has saved department $10,000. System has since been purchased by 90 percent of other departments in company.

Supervise (10) employees—secretaries (3); typists (4); and clerical workers (3). Advise staff on level of work and goals of the department. Examine work of staff and make recommendations for improvement or change.

Maintain quality of work done in department. Meet with staff supervisors in other departments to coordinate work efforts.

WORD PROCESSING SUPERVISION

Supervised and coordinated the activities of 12 word processing specialists in word processing department. Responsible for the work of 20 managers. Responsible for the output of these word processing specialists in preparing correspondence, records, and reports. Assigned tasks to each staff member. Coordinated the unit's operation and did overall planning for handling of work. Trained new employees. Devised "stress-management break" for employees that reduced eye and back strain and other work-related problems.

EDUCATION:

1983–Present	UPT Business Academy, Marietta, Illinois. Currently working toward associate degree in secretarial science (word processing specialty). Have 40 credits in courses such as administrative assistant I and II and fundamentals of word processing.
1980	Allstate Business School, Marietta, Illinois. Completed certificate program in word processing.
1971–1973	Allstate Business School, Marietta, Illinois. Received certificate in secretarial studies.
1968–1971	Marietta High School, Marietta, Illinois. Received high school diploma.

SPECIAL SKILLS:

Typing (80 WPM), Gregg shorthand (80 WPM), knowledge of IBM word processing system (PC) and IBM Memorywriter; knowledge of duplicating machines, calculators, and adding machines.

REFERENCES:

Furnished upon request.

Doesn't Deloris's "after" résumé better explain her duties? Her new résumé is results-oriented and explains her on-the-job accomplishments. For example, Deloris writes, "researched, developed, and recommended purchase of telecommunications system that has saved department $10,000." This impressive statistic immediately tells a prospective employer that Deloris has desirable qualities, and he or she may think, "Maybe she will save us some money."

Figure 9 shows that Linda Pearl is a public relations director for a theater company. She wants a public relations directorship in the theater or a related area and uses the chronological résumé. Linda has a steady work history in public relations and with another theater company. However, she has told only half the story of her job duties.

FIGURE 9
Focus on Results: "Before" Résumé

Linda Pearl
9476 Venice Blvd.
Los Angeles, California 90063
(203) 367-8597

3/80–Present

Hollywood Hills Repertory Co., Los Angeles, California.

Public Relations Director

Responsible for all of the company's public relations. Met with and dealt with the press. Authored and distributed press releases. Handled department's budget. Supervised staff of 2. Handled all promotional tours of company's executives.

9/78–3/80	Lenny Kamart Associates, Los Angeles, California.
	Publicity Specialist
	Responsible for the placement of clients on local and national radio and television programs and in national and local magazines. When clients had national tours, arranged for interviews with local press and radio and television shows. Made press kits for clients.
9/76–9/78	Paris Theater Company, Los Angeles, California.
	Office Manager
	Handled administrative responsibilities including typing correspondence and answering phones.
4/75–9/78	Rams Department Store, Los Angeles, California.
	Secretary
	Handled secretarial duties for advertising manager. Answered phones and typed correspondence.

EDUCATION:

California School of Technology, Los Angeles, California. (1 year)

MEMBERSHIP:

Publicity Club of Los Angeles
Public Relations Society of America

She went to college for one year, but she didn't put her college major or the thirty credits received on this résumé. She has also forgotten the "special training" that she took in public relations through the Public Relations Society of Los Angeles. And she hasn't included awards and honors in the field. Many of these things Linda has simply forgotten. This is why remembering is the best exercise for résumé writing.

In Linda's "after" résumé (Figure 10), she has expanded her job duties and made it results-oriented. For example, "coordinated recent public relations campaign that resulted in 45 stories in national publications like the *New York Times, USA Today,* and *People.*" Any prospective employer would want a person who had Linda's capabilities in handling the local and national press. Most public relations people must have a good rapport with the media and be able to place stories in various publications. By focusing on her accomplishments or "results," Linda is able to show an impressive list of media contacts.

FIGURE 10
Focus on Results: "After" Résumé

Linda Pearl
9476 Venice Blvd.
Los Angeles, California 90063
(203) 367-8597

3/80–Present	Hollywood Hills Repertory Co., Los Angeles, California.
	Public Relations Director
	Responsible for the planning and coordination of the public relations program for the theater. Compile and write all press releases. Coordinated recent public relations campaign that resulted in 45 stories in national

publications like the *New York Times*, *USA Today*, and *People* and television appearances by theater personnel on "Hour Magazine" and "Good Morning L.A."

Coordinate all public relations events for theater. Recent events "An Evening Tribute to the Hollywood Hills Repertory" netted $25,000. Also developed "Alumni Week," where former "famous" students donated time and talent to a week of plays.

Supervise staff of 2: associate public relations director and assistant public relations director. Direct public relations activities of staffers, such as contacting media; sorting, copying, and distributing press clips; and maintenance of public relations file.

Responsible for $110,000 budget. Saved theater $12,000 by reducing costs and instituting controls.

9/78–3/80

Lenny Kamart Associates, Los Angeles, California.

Publicity Specialist

Responsible for the placement of clients on local and national television shows. Placed clients on shows like the "Phil Donohue Show," "Today," "AM America," and "CBS Morning Show." Arranged national publicity tours for clients. Articles appeared in such local papers as the *Los Angeles Times*, the *Daily News*, the *Chicago*

(continued)

Sun Times. Increased visibility of clients by 60 percent.

9/76–9/78   Paris Theater, Los Angeles, California.

Manager

Responsible for preparation of all staff biographies, photographs, and fact sheets. Assembled press kits for staffers and actors. Collected and filed press clips about theater and staff. In charge of running office smoothly.

EDUCATION:

9/75–8/76   California School of Technology, Los Angeles, California.

Majored in theater. Completed 30 credits.

SPECIAL TRAINING:

1980   Public Relations Society of Los Angeles, Los Angeles, California.

Received certificate in fundamentals of public relations and publicizing a theater company.

MEMBERSHIP:

Publicity Club of Los Angeles; Public Relations Society of America

AWARDS AND HONORS:

1983   Awarded Public Relations Award from the Los Angeles Women's Media Club.

REFERENCES:

Furnished upon request.

She is also able to expand on her supervisory abilities. Since she wants another public relations directorship, the ability to supervise is very important. Her ability to manage a $110,000 budget is something crucial that an employer would want to know. By mentioning this, she may be able to land a position where she will manage a larger budget. In these belt-tightening days, a prospective employer would want to see a job seeker's experience with budget management and the size of the budget, as well as the savings to an organization.

Charlotte Key has worked in the field of bookkeeping and wants to get a better position in the field. She has chosen the chronological résumé, but might benefit from the functional résumé because she has a spotty work history. Her first job as bookkeeping clerk for Linwood Federated Stores began in January of 1969 and lasted until September of 1975. Her next job wasn't until September of 1978. Five years elapsed before she began working at her present bookkeeping job at Mortgage Household Loans.

In Charlotte's "before" résumé (Figure 11), she has made several typical résumé-writing mistakes. First, she has put her work experience in the wrong order. She begins with her first job and ends with her last job. Next, she doesn't expand enough on her job duties. This "before" résumé will only get her a job at her present level. And she puts the names of her supervisors, which isn't necessary. Remember, if your prospective employer wants references from former supervisors, he or she will contact them or ask for letters of recommendation.

FIGURE 11
Limit to Relevant Data: "Before" Résumé

Charlotte Key
21 West Teasmont Road
Portland, Oregon 33456
(706) 456-8890

WORK EXPERIENCE:

1/69–9/75	Linwood Federated Stores, Portland, Oregon.
	Bookkeeping Clerk
	Kept records of financial transactions for Linwood Federated Stores. Put information on ledgers. Used adding machine and calculator. Supervisor, Mrs. Linda Taylor, head bookkeeper.
9/78–10/80	Acme Retail Center, Portland, Oregon.
	Bookkeeper
	Kept records of transactions in account journals. Recorded sales slips, invoices, check stubs, and inventory records. Balanced books. Figured employees' wages from records. Supervised 2 people. Supervisor, Mr. John Thomas, comptroller.
1/85–Present	Mortgage Household Loans, Portland, Oregon.
	Bookkeeper II
	Kept records of transactions. Responsible for calculating wages of employees. Balances books. Supervisor, Miss Deborah Lacy, manager, bookkeeping department.

EDUCATION:

9/67   Portland High School, Portland, Oregon.

IMPORTANT DATA:

Birthdate: May 6, 1950
Divorced; three children, ages 3, 7, and 9
Weight: 145 pounds
Height: 5'6"

HOBBIES:

Baking cookies and pies.

REFERENCES:

Miss Deborah Lacy, manager, bookkeeping
Mortgage Household Loans
87 Hale Drive
Portland, Oregon

Mr. John Thomas, comptroller
Acme Retail Center
Loomis Mall
Portland, Oregon

Reverend Sam Miller, pastor
South Hadley Methodist Church
Portland, Oregon

Charlotte has also forgotten to put her college work in the résumé. She thought that because her accumulated credits were "only" 30 it was unnecessary to put them down. Like many women without college degrees, she was ashamed that she hadn't completed her course work. Yet, she took two very important courses that will help in her bookkeeping work: Principles of Accounting I and II. In fact, accounting was her major.

Under personal data ("Important Data"), she has listed irrelevant information: References to being divorced, having three children, and her weight and height. If you put this kind of information on your résumé, you may be asked questions that shouldn't be asked in the first place—and the discussion could keep you from getting the position. For example, volunteering information about your marital status or children may open questions like, "How many more children do you plan to have?" or "Do you plan to get married again?" or "Do you think your future husband wants a wife who works?" Don't play into the prejudices of some prospective employers by putting irrelevant information on your résumé.

Charlotte also puts down a section on hobbies. Unless your hobbies relate to your future job or are worth mentioning, such as playing tennis and winning the cup at Wimbledon, forget this type of information.

Although Charlotte has had good work experience, she hasn't listed all of her duties. In her "after" résumé (Figure 12), she has listed duties and made many of them results-oriented. She has also identified the one skill area that she wants to highlight: bookkeeping. As a result, this résumé shows her to be a very competent bookkeeper.

FIGURE 12
Limit to Relevant Data: "After" Résumé

Charlotte Key
21 West Teasmont Road
Portland, Oregon 33456
(706) 456-8890 (Home)
(706) 456-9000, Ext. 34 (Office)

MAJOR SKILLS AREAS:

BOOKKEEPING

Work as Bookkeeper II for Mortgage Household Loans, the largest household loan organization in Portland. Responsible for keeping complete set of financial transaction records for 20 departments and 9 branch offices. In charge of verifying and entering details of transactions in chronological order (invoices, check stubs, requisitions, and so on). In charge of summarizing details on separate ledgers using adding and/or calculating machines. Balance books and compile reports to show statistics (cash receipts and expenditures, accounts payable and receivable, profit and loss).

Calculate wages for 200 employees for 2 semimonthly and 1 biweekly payroll. Prepare weekly payroll checks on electronic data processing system. Responsible for preparing withholding, Social Security, and other reports. Dispatch expense account to personnel and distribute FICA and federal 941, 940, and W-2 forms, and make disability, worker's compensation, union, Blue Cross, Blue Shield, and major medical insurance, and unemployment deductions. Devised system to increase efficiency of payroll calculations: introduced data processing system that has saved company $30,000 annually.

Was bookkeeper for Acme Retail Center (largest retail outlet in Portland). Was responsible for all financial transactions in department. Verified and entered transactions such as inventory, sales slips, invoices, and so on. Was responsible for supervising and coordinating the activities of 2 staff payroll clerks. Coordinated efforts of processing time cards, recording hours of work, and calculating payroll for 54 employees.

EDUCATION:

9/67–9/68	Lincoln Community College, Portland, Oregon. Took 30 credits in accounting. Courses included principles of accounting I and II.
9/65–9/67	Portland high school diploma.

REFERENCES:

Furnished upon request.

Kathy Jones is another typical woman without a college degree. She has three years of college, and was able to land a job in communications as a production assistant. She has worked as a production assistant, associate producer, and field producer. After working in the field for five years, she left for a so-called better job and has now grown tired of it. She wants to return to her former field of communications but now has six years of work experience as a researcher at a large company. How does she eliminate the research work from her résumé?

Kathy has chosen the chronological résumé (Figure 13) but the functional résumé (Figure 14) would be better for Kathy. She has had strong work experience in production, but the research work makes her résumé a hodgepodge. Since she wants to return to production work, she chooses the major work skill areas as "Production Assisting/Producing." In this résumé she is able to expound on her job duties while in production. Instead of using the limited duties in her "before" résumé ("Assisted news editors and writers in production of network radio hour news broadcasts. Researched news stories, scheduled and supervised seven employees. Handled audience inquiries,") she is able to more thoroughly explain her skills in the "after" résumé. It says that she can handle production assisting and other production jobs.

FIGURE 13
Changing Fields: "Before" Résumé

Kathy Jones
970 Rudolf Drive
Cleveland, Ohio 66789
(216) 333-8056 Home
(216) 210-6000 Office

EMPLOYMENT EXPERIENCE:

9/81   Laner Inc., Cleveland, Ohio.

                  Researcher II

                  Responsible for the research duties in
                  communications department.

12/79–8/81   Researcher I

                  Assisted Researcher II in doing research
                  for department.

5/79–10/79	Research Assistant
	Worked directly under Researcher I. Was promoted after seven months.
9/73–4/79	NBC Affiliate Network Radio News, WTLG-FM, Cleveland, Ohio.
	Production Assistant
	Assisted news editor and writers in production of network radio hourly news broadcasts. Researched news stories and scheduled and supervised 7 employees. Handled audience inquiries.
10/77	McPhearson Report, NBC Affiliate Radio News, Cleveland, Ohio.
	Associate Producer
	Responsible for coordination, editing, and researching material for 5 commentators.
11/76	NBC Election Unit.
	Field Producer
	Worked with correspondents who were covering the national presidential election Campaign '76.
	Responsible for all radio coverage from Cleveland, Ohio, on election night.
10/74–11/76	NBC Election Unit.
	Production Assistant
	Worked with producers in Cleveland involved with computer predictions during the 1974 campaign coverage.

(*continued*)

2/76–5/76 (Part-time)   Cleveland State University, Cleveland, Ohio.

                               Admissions Clerk

                               Helped with admissions for students.

EDUCATION:

1/78–Present   Cleveland State University, Cleveland, Ohio.

9/71–6/73   Case Western Reserve University, Cleveland, Ohio.

9/64–6/69   Holts School, Cleveland, Ohio.

REFERENCES:

Available upon request.

FIGURE 14
Changing Fields: "After" Résumé

Kathy Jones
970 Rudolph Drive
Cleveland, Ohio 66789
(216) 333-8056 Home
(216) 210-6000 Office

MAJOR WORK EXPERIENCE:

PRODUCTION ASSISTANT/PRODUCING

Assisted news editor and writers in production of network radio hourly news broadcasts for NBC Affiliate Radio News, Cleveland, Ohio. Identified people and news sources, nationally and internationally, to be used for broadcasts. Was responsible for keeping news scripts and log files updated. Handled listeners' inquiries about newscasts, furnished information, and made referrals.

Scheduled and supervised 7 employees for this 24-hour, 7-day-a-week operation. Performed other administrative and production duties related to hourly broadcast. Was assigned to various special projects including "Cleveland's Celebrities" and "Cleveland on the Move."

Worked as an associate producer for McPhearson Report (NBC Affiliate Radio News), Cleveland, Ohio. Worked with 5 commentators (Karl Greigson, Mindy Jameson, Linda Hudson, Frank Caperon, and Jill Regis). Responsible for all tape editing, researching accuracy or data, and meeting program deadlines.

Was field producer for NBC Election Unit. Worked with correspondents Joe Mackerell and Jody Gubble, who were following presidential candidate Carter in Cleveland, Ohio, during Campaign '76. Was responsible for all radio coverage from Cleveland on election-night broadcasts.

Assisted producers involved with computer predictions during 1974 campaign coverage throughout the country. Duties included identifying target population, contacting people by telephone, randomly selecting polling places, and coding and checking computer data accuracy. Worked with computer center staff on election night.

EDUCATION:

1/78–1/79	Cleveland State University, Cleveland, Ohio. Working to complete a bachelor of arts degree in film and communications. Total credits: 89.
9/71–6/73	Case Western Reserve University, Cleveland, Ohio.
	Completed 60 credits in communications.

SPECIAL TRAINING:

9/83–8/84	Cleveland State University, Cleveland, Ohio.
	Completed certificate program in television and radio production.

(*continued*)

PROFESSIONAL ASSOCIATIONS:

Member of Women in Communications

REFERENCES:

Furnished upon request.

Kathy also is more explicit about her college course work in her "after" résumé. Since she has 89 credits in film and communications, this should be included. In her "before" résumé, she neglected to put her major or the special training course she took in television and radio production. She also forgot to mention her membership in the professional association Women in Communications. Even though she was working in research, she still kept an active membership in this association.

Look at Marilyn Waters's "before" résumé in Figure 15. She is a secretary who wants a better-paying secretarial job with more responsibilities. She was told that her résumé should only be one page. As a result, she has left out most of her job duties. Her "before" résumé says that she doesn't do too much as a secretary other than traditional duties.

FIGURE 15
Elaborate on Your Skills: "Before" Résumé

Marilyn Waters
654 Rainbow Lane
Tampa, Florida 40063
(813) 649-7947 Home
(813) 692-3306 Office

WORK EXPERIENCE:

8/73–Present	Hadley Educational Center, Tampa, Florida.

Secretary

Prepare letters and memorandums for program. Collect and prepare reports. Review and answer correspondence. Handle calls. Take care of students' applications. Responsible for filing.

Clerk-Typist

Typed letters and answered telephones for employer.

10/69–8/73	Watson, Winston and Horowitz, Tampa, Florida.

Billing Clerk

Prepared bills, statements, and invoices. Typed contracts, memos, and letters.

9/68–10/69	Lincoln Company, Tampa, Florida.

Clerk

Recorded and mailed customers' invoices. Also answered phones.

(continued)

EDUCATION:

6/68   Tampa High School, Tampa, Florida.
                             High school diploma.

On the other hand, Marilyn's "after" résumé, shown in Figure 16, shows that she is a very capable secretary who can do administrative work. Look at her achievements: "Solely responsible for supervision of placement testing, arranging test appointments, and obtaining test results from the State Education Department. Supervised part-time and summer workers. Developed filing system that upgraded reports for over 500 clients. Created standard client letters that increased office efficiency by 50 percent." She is doing a great deal more than standard secretarial work, including supervision. Her "after" résumé highlights this.

FIGURE 16
Elaborate on Your Skills: "After" Résumé

Marilyn Waters
654 Rainbow Lane
Tampa, Florida 40063
Home Phone #(813) 649-7647
Work Phone #(813) 692-3306

WORK EXPERIENCE:

8/73–Present   Hadley Educational Center, Tampa,
                             Florida.

                             Secretary

                             Responsible for administrative duties for
                             4 career training programs.

                             Duties include assisting director by
                             coordinating office services, such as
                             preparing letters and memorandums and
                             outlining administrative procedures and
                             policies. Coordinate collection and
                             preparation of operating reports, such as

time and attendance records, terminations, new hires, transfers, and statistical records of performance data. Review and answer correspondence. Handle incoming calls regarding information for the various programs. Schedule meetings for supervisors.

Process clients' applications on CRT terminal and program them for career development classes. Solely responsible for supervision of placement testing, arranging test appointments, and obtaining test results from the state education department. Supervised part-time and summer workers. Developed filing system that upgraded records for over 500 clients. Created standard client letters that increased office efficiency by 50 percent. Participated in the various career development workshops.

8/73–10/80   *Clerk-Typist*

Typed reports, letters, forms, and schedules. Filed records and reports, posted information to clients' records. Sorted and distributed mail; answered phones.

10/69–8/73   Watson, Winston and Horowitz, Tampa, Florida.

Billing Clerk

Operated billing machine to prepare bills, statements, and invoices to be sent to customers, itemizing amounts customers owed. Other duties included typing contracts, memorandums, letters, filing, and answering phones.

(*continued*)

9/68–10/69   Lincoln Company, Tampa, Florida.

Clerk

Duties entailed recording and mailing customers' invoices, answering phones, and filing. Filmed correspondence in microfilm department.

EDUCATION:

9/84–12/84   Tampa Junior College, Tampa, Florida.

Received certificate in Word Processing I and II.

9/77–1/78   Montgomery Community College, Tampa, Florida.

Received 12 credits in business administration.

6/68   Tampa High School, Tampa, Florida.

Received high school diploma.

OFFICE SKILLS:

Shorthand, typing (60 WPM), Xerox 630 Memorywriter, Memorex 1377 CRT machine, Wang (OSI 140), and Dictaphone machine.

REFERENCES:

Furnished upon request.

Mary Henry is an administrative assistant. In her "before" résumé in Figure 17, she doesn't even bother to list her present duties but refers the reader to a job description. For her former secretarial job, she totally leaves out job duties. She assumes that a reader will know what those duties were. Next, she includes jobs at which she worked during her high school days. Unbelievably, she gives job duties for these jobs but not for the later, professional ones.

FIGURE 17
Emphasize Professional Duties:
"Before" Résumé

Mary Henry
4567 Georgia Avenue, N.W. #23
Washington, D.C. 20067
(202) 299-7875 (Home)

CAREER OBJECTIVE:

Increase responsibilities in day-to-day activities.

EDUCATION:

June 1980	Wallace Commercial High School, Arlington, Virginia. Received high school diploma.

EXPERIENCE:

February '81–Present	*Administrative Assistant* (see attached job description for duties). TRC, Inc., Arlington, Virginia.
February '80 –February '81	*Secretary*, TRC, Inc.
Summer 1978	*Sales Clerk*, Wilson's Department Store, Washington, D.C. Handled over $600 daily; responsible for selling and other retailing duties.
Summer 1977	*Secretary* (temporary position), Cambridge Pharmaceuticals. Typed, answered the phone, and greeted visitors.
Summer 1976	*Camp Counselor*, Camp Winnebago. Camp counselor to 50 girls and boys.
REFERENCES:	Furnished upon request.

After some work on her résumé, Mary produced the "after" résumé shown in Figure 18. It shows that Mary is a highly skilled administrative assistant. Her accomplishments are impressive: "Introduced new computer system to handle customers' records. This system has saved the company $18,000 by preventing lost orders, misfiling, etc. Responsible for the development and writing of weekly and monthly statistical reports. Designed new format to help speed the efficiency of reporting system.... Assume responsibility for comptroller in her absence for departmental payroll and bookkeeping matters."

FIGURE 18
Emphasize Professional Duties:
"After" Résumé

Mary Henry
4567 Georgia Avenue, N.W. #23
Washington, D.C. 20067
(202) 299-7875 Home
(202) 866-9876 Work

WORK EXPERIENCE:

February '81–Present   TRC, Inc., Bethesda, Maryland.

Administrative Assistant

Responsible for maintaining all department records, including facilities records, orders, requisition from logs, and targeted requirements. In charge of updating and maintaining department customer records.

Introduced new computer system to handle customers' records. This system has saved company $18,000 by preventing lost orders, misfiling, and so on.

Responsible for the development and writing of weekly and monthly statistical reports. Designed new format to help speed the efficiency of reporting system.

Supervise 2 staff people: one secretary and one office helper. Responsible for the coordination of office services and the output of those supervised. Train subordinates in new operating procedures and company policy.

Assist the comptroller in making payroll for sixteen employees. Assume responsibility for comptroller in her absence for department payroll and bookkeeping matters.

February '80
–February '81

Secretary

Was responsible for all secretarial duties including preparing correspondence, memoranda, and administrative reports. Scheduled appointments and handled travel and hotel accommodations for manager.

Developed form letters that increased efficiency of interdepartmental correspondence. Responsible for coordination and collection of data for statistical reports.

EDUCATION:

June 1980

Wallace Commercial High School, Arlington, Virginia.

Received high school diploma.

REFERENCES:

Furnished upon request.

Everyone can write a great résumé with a little planning. Table 11 will help you learn the dos and don'ts of résumé writing. This chart is divided into three sections: chronological, functional, and combination. Since each type is distinctive, special guidelines have been prepared to help you with each one.

TABLE 11
Résumé Checklist

Dos:	*Don'ts*
CHRONOLOGICAL RÉSUMÉ	
1. If you want to move up in your company or get a similar job in another company, use the chronological résumé.	1. Don't be too sketchy in your description of job duties.
2. If you have had a steady work history, that is, no six-month, one-year, two-year, or five- or ten-year gaps in your employment, use the chronological résumé.	2. Don't hide relevant work history at the bottom of the page or on page two.
3. Use this type if you have had jobs with progressive degrees of responsibilities.	3. Don't forget important job duties. Think of your job duties instead of your job title.
4. Assess whether your employment history or educational background should go first.	4. Don't use whole sentences to describe your work experience. Use short, brief phrases like "developed report on how to evaluate office efficiency."

TABLE 11 (*Continued*)

Dos:	*Don'ts*
5. Be sure your employment dates are correct.	5. Don't include every job you've ever had. Condense your résumé to include only relevant work experience. For example, it isn't necessary to include your summer jobs that you had as a teenager.
6. Put yourself in the place of the employer. What would he or she want in an employee for this position?	6. Don't include whole addresses for your employers or educational institutions. The employer's name and address (city and state only) will do. The same is true of educational institutions.
7. Write a résumé for every type of job that you want and highlight your job duties that are relevant to each position.	7. Don't include the names of your supervisors.
8. Write your résumé in descriptive action words.	8. Don't include the names and addresses of references. If the employer wants them, he or she will ask you to send them.
9. Make your résumé results-oriented, such as "developed a filing system that increased office efficiency by 60 percent."	9. Don't put personal data on résumés, such as date of birth, marital status, state of health, etc. It is unwise for an employer to ask most of these things. They are also unnecessary and irrelevant to your prospective job. So why include them?

(*continued*)

TABLE 11 (*Continued*)

Dos:	*Don'ts*
10. Write a job objective only if it is specific, for example, to get a sales position in a large east coast cosmetics firm.	10. Don't put hobbies on your résumé unless they have some relevance to your prospective job.
11. Make your résumé one or two pages.	11. Don't forget to put a daytime phone number on your résumé.
12. Include all relevant honors and awards.	12. Don't state salary.

FUNCTIONAL RÉSUMÉ

1. Use this type of résumé when you want to change careers or camouflage a spotty work record.	1. Don't list jobs in chronological order. Just concentrate on relevant skills.
2. Determine the skills needed for your particular position. Gear your résumé to reflect those skills. Use the *Dictionary of Occupational Titles.*	2. Don't use whole sentences to describe your job duties.
3. Choose skill areas that are relevant. For example, if you want a job in public relations, your major skill areas might be public relations, writing, and research.	3. Don't make your résumé more than one or two pages.
4. Be sure to include any relevant volunteer, community, or civic or part-time work.	4. Don't put irrelevant information on your résumé like personal data.

TABLE 11 (*Continued*)

Dos:	*Don'ts*
5. Pick any relevant thing in your background that applies to your prospective position and highlight the skills or abilities.	5. Don't state salary on the résumé.
6. Put your relevant skills first, then education, special training, or other skills next.	
7. Think of your job duties instead of job titles.	
8. Use short, descriptive action words to describe your jobs.	
9. Make a functional résumé for each type of job that you want, such as public relations, writing, etc.	

COMBINATION RÉSUMÉ

1. Use this type of résumé when you want to change careers.	1. Don't list jobs in chronological order, only in the section for major employment.
2. Use when you want to move up, deemphasize your job title, and stress job duties.	2. Don't elaborate on your job duties in the major employment section. List your jobs in reverse chronological order and put your various job titles under your present and past employers' addresses.
3. Determine the relevant skill areas needed.	3. Don't use whole sentences to describe your duties.

(*continued*)

TABLE 11 (*Continued*)

Dos:	*Don'ts*
4. Be sure to include any relevant community, civic, or part-time work.	4. Don't put irrelevant information on your résumé like personal data.
5. Be sure to include any special training or work experience.	
6. Put your relevant skills first, then your educational training and/or special skills.	
7. Limit the combination résumé to one or two pages.	

Finally, review the questions in Worksheet 8. Before you write your résumé, make sure you can answer all the questions in this worksheet. When you have done that, you are well on your way to writing a great résumé.

WORKSHEET 8
Résumé Analysis Worksheet

1. What position do you plan to get as a result of this résumé?

   _____

   _____

2. Have you thought of the skills needed for this position? What are these skills?

   _____

   _____

3. When did you become interested in this area?

   _____

   _____

4. Can you think of any experience that led you to choose this field?

   _____

   _____

5. What things in your past may have contributed to your interest in the field?

   _____

   _____

6. What special qualities do you have that make you the best candidate for the position?

   _____

   _____

7. Do you have any job experiences that make you eligible for this position?

   _____

   _____

   _____

8. Have you taken courses in the area of your training? What are they?

_____

_____

9. Do you have any special skills that are associated with your future position?

_____

_____

10. Have you received any awards or honors in your field?

_____

_____

11. Do you belong to any professional associations or groups that are associated with your field?

_____

_____

12. What are your goals in terms of your future job or field?

_____

_____

13. Where do you see yourself in five years?

_____

_____

_____

_____

How Your Résumé Should Look

Résumés should be professionally typed. There's nothing more irritating to an employer than trying to wade through a résumé typed on a bad machine. Invest in your résumé. Hire a professional typist who uses an electric typewriter with correction capabilities. If you can find a typist who has a word processing machine, employ his or her services. You'll be able to get a variety of headings with a word processing machine. It will look more professional and be easier to read.

For the most professional look, invest $15 to $40 and have your résumé typeset. Again, you can choose from a variety of headings which give a more polished, professional look.

Regardless of the way your résumé is typed, make sure it is grammatically correct. This means proofing it before actual printing. Bad grammar and poor spelling on a résumé spell nonprofessional.

Once your résumé is proofed and typed, take it to a professional printer for offsetting or to a photocopying place. Offset printing will make your résumé look more professional. But you can do a great job with photocopying. Instead of using the regular copying paper, ask for better-quality paper. Some copying places, for example, use 100 percent rag paper or fine-quality paper with linen or parchment textures. If your copying store doesn't have better-quality paper, supply your own. Most stationery stores have fine-quality paper.

Choose paper that is white or beige. Don't use colored paper or colored ink. Most companies are very conservative, and will frown on résumés that are too gaily colored. The best rule of thumb is to stick with white or beige paper and black ink.

Your cover letter (see Chapter 7) should also be printed on the same paper. Consistency is important and adds a professional touch. Make sure each of your cover letters is individually typed. Many secretarial services will do multiple letters and print them on paper supplied by you.

7

Grabbing the Employer's Attention: Developing a Surefire Cover Letter

Your cover letter is the first document a prospective employer sees. It should be neat, carefully written, grammatically correct, and written on your best stationery. Don't send form letters—they imply that you don't care. Each letter should be individually typed and should be specifically addressed to the person in charge. Be sure to include a specific department and the position for which you are applying.

Your tailor-made cover letter should be written with the prospective employer in mind. Many employers receive hundreds of résumés and cover letters each week. Be smart and make it easier for the employer to see that you qualify for the job. Learn how to write an effective cover letter, and you will be asked for more interviews.

Cover-Letter Basics

First, decide the position for which you are applying. Never be vague about the position or the department. Be as specific as possible! For example, if you are interested in applying for a computer operator's position, give the exact title: Computer Operator

II. Then pinpoint the department: "I am interested in applying for a Computer Operator II position in your telecommunications unit."

Next, highlight the experience or training that makes you eligible for the job, for example, "I have six years of work experience as a computer operator at Viscount Industries." Then, tailor your references to your experience and training to the qualities the employer is seeking. Your career-planning homework should help with this. If you have learned, for instance, that your prospective company needs someone who specializes in a certain computer system, outline your specific experience with that particular system. And highlight any other relevant experience.

Finally, make sure that the employer knows how to get in touch with you. Include a telephone number where you are available during business hours or a place where messages can be taken.

Now let's look at some typical cover letters. Figure 19 shows a *referral cover letter*. This type of cover letter is used when you have been referred to the employer.

FIGURE 19
Referral Cover Letter

870 Winston Road
Los Angeles, California 90028
September 30, 1987

Ms. Karen Milford
Vice President
Telecommunications Unit
Amcon Teletronics
80 High Tech Road
Los Angeles, California 90031

Dear Ms. Milford:

Mr. John Eldridge of Telco Electronics asked me to write you. He informed me that you are currently looking for a Computer Operator II for your DataTronics System. I have worked for seven years as a computer operator on that system at Linton Electronics, Westbank Electric, and Madison Technologies.

My background seems well suited for your position. Mr. Eldridge told me that you are particularly interested in an efficiency expert. I have developed several operating procedures that may interest you. While at Linton, I designed a system that increased computer operations efficiency by 75 percent. I developed similar systems for Westbank and Madison and had similar results.

I would like to meet with you and discuss my employment as a Computer Operator II with your company. For your convenience, I have enclosed a copy of my résumé.

In a week, I will call your secretary to arrange an appointment. Or you may call me at (213) 655-9870.

Many thanks for your time and consideration.

Sincerely,

Mary Johnson

In the first paragraph, Mary acknowledges the person who made the referral and why it was made. Next, she explains her background and why she is suited for the position.

In the next paragraph, Mary goes into depth about her work experience. Since she knows that the employer is looking for an efficiency expert, she stresses that part of her background. She makes her work accomplishments results-oriented ("I designed a system that increased computer operations efficiency by 75 percent"). Wouldn't any employer be interested in her background? She has subtly whetted the employer's interest. She indicates that she has created similar systems for other employers.

Finally, she expresses an interest in the position and a desire for an interview and refers to the enclosed résumé. Her last sentence tells the employer that she will be getting in touch to arrange a meeting. But if the employer wants to reach her, she has included her telephone number. At the end, she thanks the employer for her time in reading the cover letter and résumé and for further consideration.

Kathy Jones (remember her from Chapter 6?) has seen a job posting at a local radio station. She uses the typical *response-to-posting* or *want-ad cover letter,* shown in Figure 20. Remember, Kathy had worked for a radio station but switched to research for a corporation. Now, she wants to return to production work. Her cover letter must complement her revised résumé (Figure 14), which highlights only her production assisting and producing skills. So she concentrates only on previous production work.

**FIGURE 20
Response-to-Posting or
Want-Ad Cover Letter**

970 Rudolf Drive
Cleveland, Ohio 66789
January 13, 1986

Ms. Roslyn Nelson, Producer
WKLT-FM
3024 Ramsam Drive
Cleveland, Ohio 66789

Dear Ms. Nelson:

While at WKLT, I saw a posting for the position of Production Assistant (memorandum #6756) and would be interested in applying for it.

My work experience includes five years of radio production at NBC Affiliate Network News in Cleveland. My experience includes:

- Production Assistant for WTLG-FM where I assisted news editor and writers in hourly news broadcasts.
- Associate Producer for the McPhearson Report, a weekly news program.
- Field Producer for coverage of the 1976 Presidential Campaign.
- Production Assistant for coverage of the 1974 local political campaign.

I have 89 credits in communications from Case Western Reserve and Cleveland State University, and have a Certificate in Television and Radio Production from Cleveland State.

I am very interested in WKLT's work, and am impressed with your programming. The position of Production Assistant seems to offer an exciting challenge and career growth. I would be very interested in talking with you about the position.

I will call your secretary in a few days to set up an appointment. Or you may call me at (216) 210-6000.

Many thanks.

Sincerely,

Kathy Jones

In the first paragraph, Kathy tells the employer how she learned about the position and that she is interested in applying for it. The second paragraph highlights her production experience. She chooses this format because it is easy to read and encompasses all of her production experience.

Next, she builds on her work experience by outlining her educational training. Notice that she includes all of her college credits and notes her completion of a certificate program in television and radio production.

Because Kathy is familiar with her prospective employer, she indicates a knowledge of WKLT's programming. She again indicates an interest in the position and its career opportunities.

In the last paragraph, she says that she will call in a few days and gives her telephone number.

Deloris Stuart (remember her from Chapter 6?) is an administrative assistant who has worked as a word processing supervisor. Her type of cover letter, shown in Figure 21, can be sent if you read about an employer in a trade or professional association journal, in a women's or general magazine, or in the newspaper. Deloris has read an article in an industry journal, *Word Processing World*, about the future employment needs of Christian Brothers.

FIGURE 21
Sample Cover Letter

916 Main Street
Marietta, Illinois 80097
December 11, 1986

Mr. John Thompson, Director
Word Processing Unit
Christian Brothers Inc.
543 Hammerston Road
Marietta, Illinois 80097

Dear Mr. Thompson:

I discovered by reading *Word Processing World* that your company is reorganizing your Word Processing Unit, and needs word processing supervisors with prior administrative experience.

I believe that I have the experience and background you want. For three years, I was the word processing supervisor for Wilson Mills. In this position, I supervised fourteen word processing specialists, who were responsible to twenty managers. Presently, I am an administrative assistant at Lincoln Textiles and supervise ten employees.

Your article also indicated that your employees suffer from many work-related health problems due to long work hours on the word processing equipment. While at Wilson, I was able to reduce the number of these types of work-related illnesses in the Word Processing Unit by developing a "stress-management break" system. This system gave employees a number of exercises that helped reduce eye strain and back problems. As a result, employee absenteeism was reduced by 60 percent.

Your unit's reorganization sounds challenging. I would like to explore the possibility of my helping your company accomplish this. For your reference, I have enclosed a copy of my résumé.

I will call you in a week to set up an appointment. Or you can reach me at (618) 355-9090 during business hours.

Many thanks for your consideration.

Sincerely,

Deloris Stuart

In the first paragraph, she explains what position she wants and where she learned about it. Next, she explains her work as a word processing supervisor, the number of employees that she has supervised, and the type of work that her unit did. Next, she addresses the prospective employer's specific need to reduce employee work-related problems by describing one of her work-related accomplishments that could help the new employer.

Finally, she indicates an interest in the company's reorganization and a desire to pursue career opportunities there. Her last sentence alerts the employer that she will be contacting him in a week and gives a number where he can reach her.

Each of these cover letters is effective. It conveys an interest in the position, a knowledge of the position or company, a brief sample of the writer's tailor-made expertise and training, and a desire to meet to explore these topics at a convenient time.

Remember, the cover letter is the first thing an employer sees from you. Make it interesting, comprehensive, and as perfect as possible.

8

Getting the Job:
Passing the Interview!

In previous chapters, you learned to polish your attitude, set your career and monetary goals, assess your interests and abilities, analyze your skills, do career homework, and write résumés and cover letters. Now, you will learn how to use this information at your important job interview.

In the last chapter, you learned how to write a cover letter to the person who can hire you. So let's say that you sent that letter along with your résumé. One or two weeks have passed, and you haven't heard anything. Remember the last line of your cover letter: "I will call you in a week or two to set up an appointment." Do it! Why be a bundle of nerves waiting for the employer to call you? Don't put yourself in a subordinate role. Find out if the employer is interested. If he or she is not, then move on to the next position.

Once you have the employer on the phone, be very direct. Refer to your letter and résumé and ask for an interview date. Some employers may try to screen you on the phone, but don't get into a lengthy discussion. Concentrate only on setting up the interview! Hopefully, the interviewer will agree to see you.

Now it's time to prepare for the interview. The best preparation for the interview is knowing yourself, your future company, and some typical interview questions. Go back to the beginning of the book and review your goals, skills, and the information about the industry and company where you want to work. Now look at the questions in Table 12, Frequently Asked Interview Questions. Go over each question and write down your answers. Writing your responses will help you commit them to memory.

TABLE 12
Frequently Asked Interview Questions

What are your long-range and short-range goals and objectives, when and why did you establish these goals, and how are you preparing yourself to achieve them?

What specific goals other than those related to your occupation have you established for yourself in the next ten years?

What do you see yourself doing five years from now?

What do you really want to do in life?

What are your long-range career objectives?

How do you plan to achieve your career goals? ·

What are the most important rewards you expect in your business career?

What do you expect to be earning in five years?

Why did you choose the career for which you are preparing?

Which is more important to you: the money or the type of job?

What do you consider to be your greatest strengths and weaknesses?

How would you describe yourself?

How do you think a friend who knows you well would describe you?

What motivates you to put forth your greatest efforts?

Why should I hire you?

(*continued*)

TABLE 12 (*Continued*)

What qualifications do you have that make you think that you will be successful in your career?

How do you determine or evaluate success?

What do you think it takes to be successful in a company such as ours?

In what ways do you think you can make a contribution to our company?

What qualities should a successful manager possess?

Describe the relationship that exists between a supervisor and those reporting to him or her.

What two or three accomplishments have given you the most satisfaction? Why?

If you were hiring for this position, what qualities would you look for in an applicant?

What college subjects did you like best? Why?

What college subjects did you like least? Why?

Do you have plans for continued study?

In what kind of work environment are you most comfortable?

How do you work under pressure?

How would you describe the ideal job for you?

Why did you decide to seek a position with this company?

What do you know about our company?

What two or three things are most important to you in your job?

Are you seeking employment in a company of a certain size? Why?

What criteria are you using to evaluate the company for which you hope to work?

Do you have a geographic preference? Why?

Will you relocate? Does relocation bother you?

TABLE 12 (*Continued*)

Are you willing to travel?

Are you willing to spend at least six months as a trainee?

Why do you think you might like to live in the community in which our company is located?

What major problems have you encountered, and how did you deal with them?

What have you learned from your mistakes?

Source: *The Northwestern Lindquist Endicott Report*, Placement Center, Northwestern University, Evanston, Illinois 60201. Reprinted with permission.

Tackling Six Typical Interview Questions

Let's see how you might tackle six of the difficult interview questions from "Frequently Asked Interview Questions":

1. What are your long-range and short-range goals and objectives, when and why did you establish these goals, and how are you preparing yourself to achieve them?

This should be easy! You have already stated your short-, medium-, and long-range goals and when you plan to achieve them (refer to Worksheet 1).

By asking this question, the interviewer wants to know what type of person you are. Are you well grounded and future-oriented with goals and plans? Or are you a happy-go-lucky person with little or no direction? When you answer this question, let the interviewer know that you know yourself and where you are going.

Your long-range goal is what you ultimately want to do. For example, you may ultimately want to move into upper management in the word and information processing department of a large firm. Tell the interviewer your exact future plans and how you plan to achieve this. By projecting this far into the future, you are letting the employer know that you care about the future and your progress in the company.

Your long-range goal may be upper management, but what are your short-range goals? You may, for example, want to begin as an entry-level word processing operator. To advance in the position, you may want to begin working on an associate degree in word processing while you are working. These would be short-range goals.

2. What do you see yourself doing five years from now?

Again, go back to Worksheet 1, Question 9a. In your answer to this question, you have indicated what you hope to be doing in five years. Tell the interviewer. Be sure to tie in your five-year career goals with your progress in the company. For example: "I plan to be a Computer Programmer III in five years. In your company, I know that the career ladder begins with the Computer Programming I position, and progresses to Computer Programmer II. In order to help me achieve my five-year goal, I am prepared to contribute my best to the company. But I also plan to take the Career Development Series for Computer Specialists course at ABC University to assist my technical knowledge of the field."

3. What do you really want to do in life?

Worksheet 1 should also be helpful in answering this. What do you really want to do with the rest of your career life? Map it out for the interviewer. Think deeply and answer this question truthfully. You may answer the question like this: "My biggest dream has been to be a secretary. But a few years ago, I became intrigued with the word processing field. I fell in love with the field and the new technological advances it offered the office. Through the use of word processing, the nature of today's workplace has been changed. In all honesty, I want to be a part of that change. The field is rapidly growing and offers many opportunities for a person like me. I would like nothing better than working as a word processing professional and contributing to this much needed career area. Ultimately, I would like to reach the top of the field. In your company, that is vice president in charge of word processing management."

By answering the question in this way, you will tell the interviewer several things. First, you are establishing a long-term interest in the field. Understandably, as technology improved, your career goals changed. Secondly, you will be indicating that you will be taking courses to prepare for the field. And lastly, you are showing a genuine excitement about the field.

4. How do you plan to achieve your career goals? (Or what position or positions in the company will help you achieve your goals?)

This interview stumper requires a great deal of thought and intensive career homework. What the question really asks is, how will you get from point A to point B. Since most job seekers are short-sighted or just interested in getting a job, this question usually throws them. Don't let this happen to you!

What is the next job you want after the present job? How would you move up into the position? Who is presently in the position, and how did he or she get there? What is the standard career path for positions of this type?

One smart job seeker, for example, found valuable career-path information about her future company by looking in a directory that listed the biographies of top company executives, and analyzed their career paths. She found that most of the top executives in her prospective company started in the sales department. Logically, she also decided to set her sights on sales.

Another way to find career-path information is to request from the company a copy of their recruiting brochure. Some brochures explain a typical career path for a given position. Or sometimes, career information from professional associations can provide typical career paths to the top. After you have reviewed this material, plot your own career path.

Don't forget to include any educational plans that will help you achieve your goals. Be sure to talk about courses that you have taken and will take in the future.

5. What do you consider to be your greatest strengths and weaknesses?

This is your opportunity to really impress the interviewer. Let's go back to your lists of skills and job duties (Worksheets 3 and 4). Review these lists and focus on possible strengths.

When the interviewer asks you this question, focus on your strengths and the skills needed for the job. Sum up your strengths like this: "My greatest strengths have always been in the areas of typing and communications. I have always been able to type very fast. My typing speed is now 80 words a minute. As a word processing specialist, it is very important to communicate well, both orally and in writing. I have taken several courses in business writing and public speaking. I know how to communicate well in both areas. In fact, my former employers have always complimented me on the clarity of my writing and oral presentations. As you know, another important skill for a word processing specialist is good grammar skills. My spelling and punctuation have always been top-notch."

This type of answer does two things: it establishes your knowledge of the necessary skills for the job, and it focuses on your skill level in needed areas.

It may also be good to include some of your job-related accomplishments. You can say something like this: "One of my best strengths is to recognize problems in the department and determine how to resolve them. For example, in my present company, we had a problem with our filing system. It took entirely too much time for the secretaries to file and retrieve information, and this kept us from doing more essential work. So I devised a system to eliminate time-consuming filing tasks. I developed a method that allowed employees to classify work quickly and to eliminate the unnecessary filing of unimportant documents and the storing of outdated materials."

You have told the interviewer that you are an employee who solves problems, and most employers want that. Although you didn't say it, you implied that you saved your company money by reducing unnecessary utilization of time. What employer wouldn't want your services?

What are your weaknesses? When asked this question, many job seekers immediately begin to talk about their job-related weaknesses. Forget about that! Concentrate only on your strengths by turning so-called weaknesses into strengths. For example, you can say: "One of my weaknesses is that I work too hard!" Or: "Although I know that I shouldn't spend so many hours thinking about the job, I do." Or you can say: "Some people consider me a workaholic. I suppose this is a weakness, but I love what I do and spend many hours doing it and thinking about it." By turning your weaknesses into strengths, you aren't giving the interviewer a chance to form a negative opinion about you.

6. What qualifications do you have that make you think that you will be successful in your career?

This question belongs in the category of "Why should I hire you?" Again, knowing your job-related accomplishments and skills will help. The interviewer wants to know exactly why you will be an asset to the company. This is no time to be shy! Many women have been taught to be shy about their accomplishments, that it isn't ladylike to brag about accomplishments and that one should never "toot one's own horn." But if you want to get the job, you must firmly and ecstatically tell of your accomplishments and skills. Put your best foot forward or lose the chance for the job. In a good firm voice say, for example, "I have had seven years as a secretary with progressive responsibilities throughout the years. I can type 80 words a minute and take dictation at 120 words a minute. I am a graduate of the

Teasdale Business School and graduated valedictorian of my class. I am very interested in word processing and have taken several seminars in the field. In order to become the best word processing professional, I plan to get an associate degree in the field. I also plan to augment my knowledge of the Wang system by learning the IBM and other systems. I am also interested in taking some computer courses to complete my knowledge of word and information processing." Then add any other job-related accomplishments that make you qualified for the position.

The key to answering this type of question is to put yourself in the place of the interviewer and to try to discover his or her needs for the position. Once you have done this, you will be able to answer this question with flying colors.

The questions in Table 12 aren't really difficult. It just takes a little thought and soul-searching to answer them properly.

After you have thought about the answers to these questions, it is now time to commit them to memory. The best way to commit interview responses to memory is to have a friend practice with you. Choose someone who is really interested in your welfare, and sincerely wants to help. Prepare a list of questions for your friend. Then arrange to meet in a place where you won't be disturbed and can talk freely. Devote at least two hours a day for a couple of days to this practice interviewing.

Another way to practice for your interview is to commit your responses from the practice interview to memory. Tape your practice interview with a tape recorder. Then on the way to work or in the evenings listen to the tape over and over. Repetition is a great way to memorize anything.

The Big Day: The Interview

You have successfully practiced for your interview and/or gone on casual interviews. It is now time for your real interview. To help prepare for your interview, you must do some things the night before. Take out your interview clothes and look them over. Make sure your blouse's buttons are sewn on and check your shoes. Are the heels in perfect condition? It's pretty bad to wake up the morning of the interview to find that your clothes aren't in tip-top condition. Attend to your interview clothes the night before and save yourself a great deal of frustration.

On the subject of clothes, know what to wear to an interview. Your career homework should give you a clue to your future company's dress codes. Is the company conservative? If so, dress accordingly. Is the company or industry fashionable? Then don't wear drab and fashionless clothes. Your clothes should reflect the company's image and style, because the object of dressing for an interview is to look the part of an employee at that company. You want to look like a team member. If your interviewer feels comfortable with you because you look like a team member, you have taken a giant step toward getting the job.

Review your notes about your prospective company. Do you know how people in the company dress? If not, talk to someone in the company. If you can't get this information, think about the image the company tries to convey.

When in doubt about makeup or jewelry, be conservative. A tastefully made-up face is a plus. Your jewelry should be simple: no dangling earrings or chunky bracelets. Simplicity is better than overdoing it.

Another thing to do the night before is to determine the best transportation route to the interview. If you will be driving, make sure you consider rush-hour traffic. Is there an alternative route that you can take? Or should you leave earlier?

Next, if you have any support information that will document your work accomplishments, put that into your briefcase. Do you have any letters, awards, or reports that will help prove you can do the job? Don't try to find these items the morning of the interview! Spend a few minutes gathering this information the night before the interview.

Finally, get a good night's sleep. There's nothing worse than walking into the interview in a bleary-eyed state. Get a good eight hours of sleep.

Be sure to arrive at the interview on time and alone. It may be hard to believe, but some people bring a friend along to interviews. Some people think they need moral support. However, this is the worst thing to do. Walk alone!

In the interviewer's office, begin immediately to establish rapport. You can comment on the beauty of the interviewer's office, but only if it is beautiful. If it isn't, the interviewer will know that you are trying to butter him or her up, and more importantly, that you're not honest.

Another great ice-breaker is commenting on something you noticed on the way to the interviewer's office. For example, say something like, "I couldn't help but notice that your company has the latest office equipment. It's also very interesting the way the employees' cubicles are arranged. Was that done for a particular reason? I was reading that this type of arrangement allows more employee creativity and productivity. Was this your reason for the arrangement? I'm fascinated with this whole area and have done some research on it."

By commenting on the office and special features, you are giving the interviewer a chance to brag about his or her company. You are also bringing some of your work interests into the conversation.

Regardless of the method you use to establish rapport with the interviewer, make sure he or she feels comfortable with you.

After the interviewer moves the conversation to you and your abilities and skills, look at him or her directly and begin to answer each question. By now, you should be more relaxed and able to handle difficult questions. Go back to the Frequently Asked Interview Questions in Table 12 and mentally go through your responses.

For further help as you tackle the interview, look at the following three tips for avoiding interview faux pas. Each represents a mistake that many job seekers make in the interview session:

1. Always be considerate of the interviewer. Remember, she or he is a person, so be respectful.

2. Don't volunteer information. Never comment on things that aren't asked of you. Too many people have lost jobs because they were too revealing. For example, one of my clients breezed through an interview. At the end, the interviewer asked her if there was anything she wanted to add. My client began, "Do you have a policy about people who have been 'locked out' of their former jobs?" The interviewer replied, "What do you mean, 'locked out'?" My client continued, "Well, it's when the company hasn't fired you, but you can't come to work either. It means that you are locked out of the building." Did my client get the job? No! Don't try to be a good samaritan in the interview situation and tell your entire life history. Answer only questions that are asked of you.

3. Don't talk negatively about your present or past employer. In the business world, bad-mouthing your present or former employer is tantamount to treason. It's something that puts you in a bad light. In every interview, say only good things about your present and former employer. Even if you were terribly unhappy with the job, there must be some aspects of it that you liked. Focus on these positive things.

You should know that there are several types of interview formats, and your interview may use any one or a combination. You should, therefore, be prepared for each type. The first type is the *question and answer* (Q & A) *interview.* In this type of interview, the interviewer has prepared a set of questions. She or he has carefully selected these questions and hopes to get certain responses from you. The interviewer generally wants to know three things:

1. Can you do the job?

2. Did your educational and work background prepare you to do the job?

3. Will you be the type of employee the company wants?

Stick to your skills and abilities and the results of your work, and you'll be on the right track. Most of the questions in a Q & A interview will be similar to the questions that you reviewed earlier in this chapter, for example, "What are your long-range career goals?"

In many ways, the Q & A interview is the easiest. You are in the interview situation with only one person, and there are a set number of questions that are asked. Review your answers to the six most typical interview questions and sail through this type of interview.

The next type of interview is the *unstructured interview*. The interviewer will ask you just a few questions about your background and personality. The questions will appear to have no structure. One could be: "Tell me about your childhood. Where were you born? And where did you go to school? What did your parents do for a living?" There may be little or no attention paid to your educational or work background, and you may begin to wonder why. Don't be fooled.

This type of interview may not seem to have any rhyme or reason, but the interviewer is learning a great deal about you. The interviewer can, for example, find out a great deal about a person by his or her likes and dislikes. Your childhood can tell a great deal about you as an adult. This type of interview subtly helps the interviewer paint a composite picture of you.

To prepare for this type of interview, review Worksheet 1, Question 1 on your childhood goals and think about your childhood interests, likes, and dislikes. Next, write a brief autobiography of yourself. Limit it to the things you want to stress in the unstructured interview. Remember, in the interview you want to be able to answer the interviewer's questions in depth. So prepare for it!

The *group interview* is another type of interview and can be very stressful. You must face a group of three or more people. Sometimes, group interviews can include as many as ten people. In this interview, everyone must give you a stamp of approval.

Since you probably won't have any prior indication that you'll be meeting with a group of people, don't be intimidated by a large group. Situate yourself where you can have full eye contact with each group member. Inevitably, there will be one group member who appears to dislike you. Ignore this person and focus on the people who are radiating more positive energy. Once you have won over the rest of the group, the disagreeable member will probably join the rest or be outvoted.

The group will want to know your educational and work background and what you can offer the team. Now is the time to really shine. Focus on your skills and abilities and job-related accomplishments. Remember, the group is interested in getting the best team member. Show them that you have done your homework and understand some of their needs. If you can relax, this type of interview can be a cinch.

Successive interviews are several interviews with different people, who have increasing authority in the company. You may have two, three, or four of these interviews, and each interviewer must give you a stamp of approval. These interviews can take place over one or more days.

Hopefully, your successive interviews will take place on separate days. This will allow you to think about your responses in the first interview, and improve them for the second or following interviews. It will also give you a chance to find out who the second interviewer is and get tidbits about him or her from your source inside the company. Is the person friendly or aloof? What type of employee does he or she like and want? What do his or her employees think of him or her? The more information that you can learn about your next interviewer, the better you can prepare for the interview.

Remember, each successive interview is more important than the last. Don't get to your last interview and ruin your chances. Build on each interview by reviewing; getting more information; and expanding your description of your skills, abilities, and job-related accomplishments.

By now, you have some idea of how to conduct yourself in the interview situation. To help you further, look at some reasons that people don't get jobs listed in Table 13. If you have properly prepared for your interview, you should be able to overcome these obstacles. Also study Interviews Dos and Don'ts in Table 14.

TABLE 13
Reasons People Do Not Get Jobs

Poor personality and manner; lack of poise; poor presentation of self; lack of self-confidence; timid, hesitant approach; arrogance; conceit

Lack of goals and ambition; failure to show interest; uncertainty and indecisiveness about the job in question

Lack of enthusiasm and interest; no evidence of initiative

Poor personal appearance and careless dress

Unrealistic salary demands; more interest in salary than in opportunity; unrealistic about promotion to top jobs

Poor scholastic records without reasonable explanation for low grades

Inability to express oneself well; poor speech habits

Lack of maturity; no leadership potential

Lack of preparation for the interview (failure to get information about the company and consequent inability to ask intelligent questions)

Lack of interest in the company and the type of job offered

Lack of extracurricular activities without good reason

Attitude of "what can you do for me"

Objection to travel; unwillingness to relocate to branch offices or plants

Source: *The Northwestern Lindquist Endicott Report*, Placement Center, Northwestern University, Evanston, Illinois 60201. Reprinted with permission.

TABLE 14
Interview Dos and Don'ts

Dos	*Don'ts*
1. If you get no response to your cover letter and résumé, call the interviewer. Set up an interview.	1. Don't let an interviewer screen you on the phone. Your object is to set up an interview, not to be screened out of one.
2. Practice and rehearse for your interviews with a friend. Use the six typical interview questions and the frequently asked interview questions (Table 12) in practice interviews.	2. Don't leave things to chance. Prepare!
3. If possible, get a video camera and tape a mock interview.	3. Don't stay up the night before an interview. Get a good night's sleep.
4. Call networking resources for inside information about your future department, company, and, most importantly, the interviewer.	4. Don't go to an interview when you're sick. Reschedule.
5. Schedule your interviews according to your internal "clock," for example, "morning" people should schedule morning interviews.	5. Don't be late for any reason.

(*continued*)

TABLE 14 (Continued)

Dos	Don'ts
6. Decide the best interview clothes by reviewing your career and networking notes about the company. Match your wardrobe to the company's style and image. Dress the part.	6. Don't chew gum or eat candy or breath mints.
7. The night before the interview, check your clothes and shoes. Make sure they are in tip-top shape.	7. Don't smoke.
8. Put together a portfolio or spiral-bound book with samples of your work.	8. Don't wear dark glasses, hats, or other things that will obstruct your eyes.
9. The night before, check traffic and transportation patterns. You don't want to be late because of transportation delays.	9. Don't wear sneakers.
10. On the morning of the interview, eat a good breakfast. You'll probably think better after a good meal.	10. Don't bring a friend or husband to the interview for moral support.
11. Arrive early for the interview.	11. Don't take your coat or hat into the interviewer's office. Leave it in the hall closet or ask the receptionist where you can hang it.
12. Arrive alone!	12. Don't look nervous or act anxious.

TABLE 14 (*Continued*)

Dos	*Don'ts*
13. Greet the interviewer with enthusiasm.	13. Don't interrupt the interviewer.
14. Observe things about the company or office on your way to the interviewer's office.	14. Don't volunteer negative information about yourself.
15. Establish a rapport with the interviewer. Focus on his or her interests or things about the company.	15. Don't bad-mouth your present or former employer.
16. Focus on your skills, abilities, education and work history, strengths, and work-related accomplishments.	16. Don't be thrown by the different types of interviews: unstructured, group, etc.
17. Be positive about yourself, the position, and the company.	
18. Be positive about your present or past employer.	
19. Be knowledgeable about the company (information you have gained from the annual report and other sources).	
20. Know how to deal positively with each type of interview, such as unstructured, question and answer, etc.	
21. Turn your weaknesses into strengths.	
22. Be confident and self-assured.	

Now, let's look at two areas that we haven't discussed: salary and relocation. How do you handle salary negotiation? Unfortunately, most women have a problem with it. Somewhere along the line, we were told it isn't ladylike to talk about, to want, or to ask for money. More importantly, we weren't told anything about salary negotiation.

Let's look at how much money you want to make in one, five, ten, fifteen, or twenty-five years or by age sixty-five. Review your answers in Worksheet 2. Now look at your career homework and networking notes. What are the current salaries paid in your field or position? What can a person with your experience and education expect to make?

Now review your job accomplishments in Worksheet 7. What did you contribute to your present or former employers or in your unpaid work? How much money did you save your company by developing that new filing system? Place a monetary value on your accomplishment. If you saved time for your company, for example, you saved the firm money. Think of your accomplishments in terms of a monetary contribution to your companies and/or volunteer organizations (past and present).

Since most women are underpaid, let's try to build up your present salary. Do you have an extensive benefits package (medical, dental, optical, and insurance benefits)? If so, what is it worth? If you're not sure, check with your personnel department or look at your benefits booklet. What is your paid sick, vacation, and personal time worth? Do you get special job perks (expense account, company car, mileage allowance, and so forth)? What is that worth in dollars and cents? Do you receive paid educational benefits or reimbursements? That is worth money.

When you combine your salary and benefits, doesn't your salary take a sudden leap upward? Isn't an $18,000 job worth $23,000? During salary negotiations, your total salary package is what you should concentrate on. When asked your present salary, give your combined salary package by saying, "My salary package equals $23,000."

When should you bring up salary? Talk salary after the interviewer makes an offer. But remember, the interviewer may want to get you at the lowest price. It's to the employer's advantage to get employees for the least amount of money. Don't buy this! An interviewer will usually offer you the lowest salary in the salary range.

But you have done your career homework and received salary information from your networking sources. You know the salary range and aren't about to be fooled into taking the lowest salary. Assess what you're worth and ask for it. Start high and negotiate down.

For example, you know that the average word processing specialists' salary range is from $19,000 to $21,000. But you've learned that your prospective company pays more because of its emphasis and the importance it places on word processing. Your source inside the company has told you that a beginning Word Processing Specialist I can command beginning salaries of $20,900. However, employees that are sought after can get beginning salaries of $23,000. You are presently making $19,000, but with your benefits package, your salary is worth $23,000. Of course, you want a raise, so you start the negotiations at $25,000 and negotiate down.

If you are still a little apprehensive about asking for what you are worth, go back and look at your skills, abilities, and work-related accomplishments. Wouldn't any employer want you? Wouldn't you be an asset to any company? Think about this, and go into the negotiating session with confidence.

The key to good salary negotiation is being realistic about the salary range and having the confidence to ask for what you want. Don't ask for $40,000 when the job is only worth $20,000. Keep within the range, and you'll come out a winner.

Relocation is always a very sticky area for anyone, particularly a woman. If you are single, relocating may not be a big problem. But married women have husbands and sometimes children to consider. If you're married, before you turn down a relocation possibility that can advance your career, talk it over with your husband and children. You may find that they are more willing to move than you thought.

More and more women will have to consider relocation. There are some jobs and some companies that require relocation, in order for employees to progress satisfactorily. If you're unable to relocate, be honest with the interviewer. If relocation is a real problem, just steer clear of companies and jobs that will require you to build in relocation for career movement.

After-Interview Manners

After each interview, it is good business to send a thank-you note. It shows that you are courteous and professional. More importantly, it gives you an opportunity to reiterate some of the points you made in the interview.

Employers' memories can be short. They may generally know that you were impressive, but you must refresh their memories about the details. Let the after-interview thank-you letter do this and add additional points for you. For example, you may say: "Thank you very much for an informative interview. Let me stress that working for your company will be an exciting and challenging opportunity. As we discussed, I feel confident that I will be able to handle the efficiency problems experienced in your department. I feel that my background in efficiency control will be a great asset to your department. I have already thought of one or two ways that I could be of service," and so on.

After-interview thank-you notes should be written on your best stationery. For best effect, use the same paper used for your résumé and cover letter.

After the letter is sent, determine when to contact the employer. For example, if it has been three weeks since your interview, you are perfectly correct to contact the interviewer to find out your status. Tell the person that you have had some other "offers" and would like to know your status with his or her company. This will help the employer deal squarely with you. Either you have the job or you don't!

Remember, employers are people too, and many don't like hurting other people's feelings. So, rather than turn you down over the phone or in writing, they dread and avoid having to reject anyone. You must help them overcome this. After all, it's your life and livelihood that's at stake. So get an answer!

If the interviewer says that you didn't get the job, don't pout. Ask him or her the reason. Since you should think of every interview as a learning experience, you simply want to know ways to improve yourself for the next interview.

Even if you are turned down on more than one occasion, don't give up hope. With each experience, you are learning and improving yourself. All that accumulated knowledge will eventually lead to a position.

Good luck!

PART TWO

Bread and Butter Careers for Women without College Degrees

9

High Technology Careers

Computer Service Technicians:
Troubleshooting in High Tech

Computers are everywhere: in homes, offices, hotels and motels, car rental agencies, colleges and universities, grocery stores, telecommunications networks, and so on. The computer age has taken us by storm and created some booming opportunities for its specialists. One such specialist is the computer service technician who installs, tests, and keeps computers in good working order. For this vital service, she is handsomely paid.

Many women consider computer service technician work "dirty work" or "man's work." Forget about old stereotypes! This is a field that has many opportunities for the woman who wants to move ahead and work in a well-paid, challenging position. So, let's put aside our own self-imposed image of this career area and move into these lucrative positions.

U.S. Department of Labor, Bureau of Labor Statistics, *Occupational Outlook Handbook*, 1986.

What does a computer service technician (also called a field engineer or customer engineer) do? This professional must keep the computer system's equipment (central processing unit, remote terminals, tape and disk storage units, and high-speed printers) in tip-top shape. She checks for defective or malfunctioning equipment and adjusts, cleans, and oils mechanical and electromagnetic parts. And she is a troubleshooter.

Computer service technicians can also help install new equipment by laying cable, hooking up electrical connections, and correcting any problems. And they are usually adept at handling customer complaints and problems.

Educational Paths

Although most employers prefer computer service technicians with some post–high school technical training (one or two years of basic electronics), it is possible to get on-the-job training for this position. If you have a high school background that includes math, physics, and electronic courses, it is possible to land a computer service technician training position. Once hired, your training program will usually last three to six months. In this on-the-job training program, you will learn elementary computer theory, computer math, and circuitry theory. Outside the classroom, you will get hands-on experience with the equipment.

Afterward, you must take an additional six months to two years of on-the-job training under the supervision of experienced technicians. And after you start working independently, you should continuously update your knowledge of the field, because of the rapidly changing technology.

Even though you can gain employment without having technical training, you can increase your chances for employment and advancement by enrolling in a one- or two-year course in computer repair or electronics and electrical engineering at a technical school or junior or community college.

Job Outlook

The U.S. Department of Labor, Bureau of Labor Statistics, predicts: "Employment for computer service technicians is expected to grow much faster than the average for all occupations through the mid-1990s." As computer technology expands, there will be an increased need for technicians to install and keep equipment correctly functioning.

Professional Associations

For more information, write to firms that use computers (manufacturing and insurance companies, banks, data processing organizations, etc.)

In addition, minority women can write to:

Black Data Processing Associates
P.O. Box 7466
Philadelphia, PA 19101

Salary Information

Full-time computer service technicians made median annual salaries of $26,700 in 1986. The low 10 percent made $15,800; the middle 50 percent made from $21,300 to $34,400 and the top 10 percent made more than $40,000 per year.

Skills Needed by a Computer Service Technician

Ability to:

1. Install, maintain, and test computer equipment
2. Know all about computer equipment

3. Troubleshoot and locate problems

4. Repair equipment

5. Deal with the public

6. Promote goodwill for the company

7. Travel from place to place

8. Schedule and keep appointments

9. Keep records of repair

10. Keep time and expense reports

11. Keep inventory reports

12. Work alone

13. Keep pace with technology

14. Act during emergencies

15. Analyze

16. Make decisions

17. Determine

18. Discover

19. Follow through

20. Investigate

21. Listen

22. Handle customers' complaints

23. Solve problems

24. Recognize problems

25. Observe

*A Computer Service Technician Must Also Have
the Following Qualities:*

1. Good vision

2. Good color perception

3. Good hearing

4. Pleasant personality

5. Good appearance

6. Patience

7. Manual dexterity

Computer Operators: Keepers of the Machines

As this society moves ahead into the high technology revolution, computers are becoming permanent fixtures in offices and homes. As computer use continues to expand, so does the field's employment opportunities. In fact, the U.S. Department of Labor says that "computer careers (computer service technicians, systems analysts, programmers, and operators) are among the fastest growing occupations, and computer operators work in the fourth fastest growing occupation."

What does a computer operator do? She is the overall monitor of computer operations. Her three basic functions include: setting controls on the computer or peripheral equipment according to the programmer's operating instructions for a particular job, loading the machine's input (cards, tapes, or disks), and monitoring the computer console to determine proper running or malfunctions.

As a computer operator, you will work for a manufacturer, bank, insurance company, college or university, wholesale or re-

U.S. Department of Labor, Bureau of Labor Statistics, *Occupational Outlook Handbook*, 1986.

tail company, or a computer company. You will perform your duties in a comfortable work environment, because computers must be housed in well-ventilated environments. And you may have to work night shifts, because many companies run computers 24 hours a day.

If you want to advance in this exciting field, you can move up to a computer operations supervisory position. Or some computer operators become programmers.

Educational Paths

Most employers will consider high school graduates for computer operators' positions. However, most want candidates to have some experience in the field. Other employers will give new employees on-the-job training, which usually lasts several months.

You can also receive training in computer operations at high schools, private computer schools, public and private vocational schools, business schools, or community or junior colleges. Some businesses are also now offering weekend seminars for high school graduates.

If you work as a cathode-ray tube (CRT) operator or in some other clerical position, you may be eligible for transfer to a computer operator's position. To help you achieve this, you may want to get some additional education by enrolling in one or two computer operations courses at a junior or community college.

Job Outlook

The U.S. Department of Labor, Bureau of Labor Statistics, says, "Employment of computer and peripheral equipment operators is expected to rise much *faster* than the average for all occupations through the mid-1990s." The predicted increase will be due to the increased use of computers in the work world.

Professional Associations

For more information, write to firms that use computers (manufacturing and insurance companies, banks, data processing organizations, etc.)

In addition, minority women can write to:

Black Data Processing Associates
P.O. Box 7466
Philadelphia, PA 19101

Salary Information

Full-time computer operators made median annual salaries of $15,600 in 1986. The middle 50 percent earned from $12,000 to $21,600, and the top 10 percent earned more than $28,000 per year.

Skills Needed by a Computer Operator

Ability to:

1. Monitor computer machinery
2. Follow instructions
3. Know computer's peripheral equipment
4. Set up equipment
5. Concentrate
6. Troubleshoot
7. Locate problems
8. Work independently or with little supervision
9. Use independent judgment

10. Feel comfortable with machines

11. Follow through

12. Get the job done

13. Anticipate problems

14. Coordinate activities

15. Deal with pressure

16. Make decisions

17. Evaluate

18. Inspect

19. Investigate

20. Listen effectively

21. Observe

Word Processing Specialists: Information Processors

Word processing has become as familiar as apple pie to office workers everywhere. Its equipment has freed these workers from boring, repetitive typing tasks by reducing the time needed for this work. With word processing machines, operators can now more quickly do duplicate letters or documents, correct and edit documents and reports without retyping pages of work, sort material for future retrieval, and so forth.

Word processing is a system that uses specialized workers (word processing specialists) to create documents by using automated office equipment, called word processing machines, or computers

---

U.S. Department of Labor, Bureau of Labor Statistics, *Occupational Outlook Handbook*, 1986.

with word processing capabilities. These word processing systems are used by many companies and institutions: insurance companies, educational institutions, business firms, manufacturers, utility companies, law firms, airlines, government agencies, and so on. And word processing equipment has just about replaced traditional electronic typewriters in the workplace.

As a word processing specialist, you can work in a variety of positions including that of word processing manager, word processing specialist, administrative secretary, correspondence secretary, word processing secretary or operator, word processing trainee, typing specialist, or communications specialist. By having skills like the ability to type 60 to 100 words per minute and excellent vocabulary, spelling, and grammar and the ability to solve problems plus training in the field, you will have the best employment opportunities. These opportunities include working in traditional nine-to-five positions, free-lancing for companies in the evenings or on weekends, or owning a business.

Word processing has created new career possibilities for administrative assistants, secretaries, and other office workers by expanding the career ladder for these workers. As a result, word processing is one of the most sought-after careers.

Educational Paths

Some office workers learn word processing on the job; others are trained at junior or community colleges, continuing education programs at four-year colleges, employment agencies, computer manufacturing companies, night high schools, or with private instructors. Some programs last only a week; others are year-long programs. There are even two-year associate degree programs given at junior or community colleges and business institutions.

Before deciding on the best program for you, determine your long-range career goals. For example, if you want to remain in the field and ultimately move into managerial positions, you might consider getting the associate degree. If you just want to learn how to operate the equipment, you might consider taking a short-term program given at a junior or community college, business institute, or night high school or by a computer manufacturer. If you want to move out of your present position into word processing, you might consider taking a year-long program that includes courses in English composition, oral communication, typing, concepts of word processing, writing for business, administration of word processing centers, and simulation of a word processing department.

You should also make sure that your prospective educational institute will prepare you properly. Will you be trained on equipment that is widely used by companies? What is the institution's placement rate? What are its graduates doing? What type of certificate, diploma, or degree will you receive? What is its worth in the marketplace? What skills will you learn?

Job Outlook

The *Occupational Outlook Handbook Quarterly* (U.S. Department of Labor, Spring 1984), says that word processing is "one of the fastest growing fields," and that the best employment opportunities are with law firms, health agencies or hospitals, insurance companies, and banks.

Professional Association

For more information, write to:

Professional Secretaries Association International
2440 Pershing Road
Kansas City, MO 64108

Salary Information

According to a survey by the Administrative Management Society, word processing operators (in the private sector) made average yearly salaries of $14,000 to $17,400 in 1985.

Free-lancers and business owners made more. In fact, in large metropolitan cities like New York, free-lancers make $8.00 an hour and over. Business owners command as much as $5.00 a page in large metropolitan areas.

Skills Needed by a Word Processing Specialist

Ability to:

1. Type 60 to 100 WPM
2. Communicate orally and in writing
3. Operate word processing equipment
4. Be accurate
5. Read and interpret documents
6. Be resourceful
7. Be independent
8. Be dependable
9. Follow through
10. Use people-management skills
11. Work under pressure
12. Meet deadlines for large amounts of work
13. Do assigned tasks
14. Sit for long periods of time
15. Concentrate

16. Follow directions

17. Classify information

18. Coordinate work efforts

19. Edit

20. Endure long hours of work

21. Examine documents

22. Explain work to others

23. Proofread work and correct errors

24. Do detail work

25. Initiate

26. Locate information

27. Retrieve information from storage

28. Observe

29. Organize

30. Appraise situations

31. Analyze

32. Use good English skills: grammar, spelling, and punctuation

10

Health Careers

Licensed Practical Nurses: Helping the Sick and Infirm

Many little girls want to be nurses. Heroine Florence Nightingale struck a responsive chord in many girls, and they envisioned donning white and rushing out to help save the world. As many girls grew into women, their original career dreams also grew. The dignity and job security of the nursing field became symbols of success.

Although nursing offers many career alternatives, being a licensed practical nurse is an exciting career challenge. It gives you an opportunity to join the nursing field as a needed health worker.

As a licensed practical nurse (LPN), you will join the health team of physicians, registered nurses (RNs), and nursing aides to deliver patient care. You will assist physicians and RNs in examining patients. You will also be responsible for a great deal of patient care: taking and recording temperatures, giving certain types of medicines, helping patients bathe and groom themselves, and changing dressings. But you will also help convalescing patients feel good about themselves and help them on the way to recovery.

U.S. Department of Labor, Bureau of Labor Statistics, *Occupational Outlook Handbook*, 1986.

Some LPNs specialize in certain areas like working in the intensive care unit or recovery room. Some help with the delivery, care, and feeding of babies. Some supervise hospital attendants and nursing aides.

Other LPNs work in private duty, giving care to the homebound sick. They also help prepare meals and assist patients with other needs.

Most LPNs work in hospitals, but some are employed by nursing homes, temporary health agencies, and private physicians. Others are self-employed.

Educational Paths

As the name implies, licensed practical nurses must be licensed in all states and the District of Columbia. For licensing, you must complete a state-approved training program and pass a written examination. The high school graduate should take a state-approved program (usually one year) to qualify for taking the licensing examination. Although high school graduates are preferred for acceptance in training programs, this varies.

You can take a state-approved licensed practical nurses' training program at trade, technical, or vocational schools. Some are offered at junior or community colleges, hospitals, or health agencies.

In these training programs, you will learn nursing concepts and principles, anatomy, physiology, medical-surgical procedures, pediatrics, obstetrics, psychiatric nursing, administration of drugs, nutrition, first aid, and community health. You must also have supervised clinical experience, usually in a hospital.

If you want to advance in the field, you may have an opportunity to become a registered nurse. Many licensed practical nurses' training programs are now structured so that graduates can eventually go on to registered nurses' educational programs.

Job Outlook

"Employment for licensed practical nurses is expected to rise at the same rate as all occupations through the 1990s," says the *Occupational Outlook Handbook*. As the need for more qualified health professionals grows and as the population lives longer, there will be a need for licensed practical nurses. Employment opportunities will be best in nursing homes.

Professional Associations

For a list of state-approved training programs, contact:

National League for Nursing
10 Columbus Circle
New York, NY 10019

For career information about the field, contact:

National Federation of Licensed
   Practical Nurses, Inc.
P.O. Box 11038
Durham, NC 27703

In addition, minority women can write to:

National Black Nurses Association
1011 North Capitol, NE
Washington, D.C. 20002

Salary Information

According to the National Federation of Licensed Practical Nurses, in 1987 LPNs made average annual salaries of $7.50 to $15.00 an hour, depending on location and extra training.

Skills Needed by a Licensed Practical Nurse

Ability to:

1. Learn technical knowledge regarding nursing
2. Take and record temperatures
3. Change dressings
4. Administer certain drugs
5. Assist in examining patients
6. Supervise others, like nursing aides
7. Provide care
8. Teach families simple nursing procedures
9. Operate equipment
10. Stand on feet for long periods of time
11. Follow through
12. Follow directions
13. Appraise situations
14. Keep records
15. Assess situations
16. Communicate orally
17. Counsel
18. Make decisions
19. Dispense
20. Distribute
21. Endure
22. Explain
23. Help others

24. Help others improve

25. Motivate and keep morale up

26. Inspire

27. Inspect

28. Listen

29. Work with public

30. Monitor

31. Observe

32. Organize

33. Recognize problems

34. Make recommendations

35. Help rehabilitate

36. Schedule

37. Summarize reports

38. Work on a team

39. Be understanding

Physical Therapist Assistants: Body Reshapers

Create a career in the nation's seventh fastest growing occupation. In fact, the *Occupational Outlook Handbook* predicts the projected growth for assistant physical therapists will be "much faster than average."

What is a physical therapist assistant? They work under the su-

---

U.S. Department of Labor, Bureau of Labor Statistics, *Occupational Outlook Handbook, 1982–1983.*

pervision of physical therapists, who help accident victims; handicapped children; stroke victims; and those with multiple sclerosis, cerebral palsy, nerve injuries, amputations, fractures, and arthritis by planning and administering treatment to restore their bodily functions. An accident victim who has lost the ability to walk is given a plan of treatment to help her walk again. A woman who has lost the use of one hand after a stroke learns with the help of physical therapy to use it again. An amputee learns how to function without a limb.

Along with the physical therapist, the physical therapist assistant is part of the health team that helps a patient better function. A physical therapist assistant's role is largely determined by state licensing regulations, the health facility's policies, the supervising physical therapist's direction, and the patient's needs.

Patience and sensibility are two traits needed by physical therapist assistants. Sometimes it's a long haul to patient recovery, and there are bound to be frustrating moments. Patiently and with sensitivity, the physical therapist assistant must help the patient keep going and not become discouraged. In fact, a physical therapist assistant's positive attitude can help combat the patient's desire to give up.

As a physical therapist assistant, your duties may include helping the physical therapist administer and evaluate tests, train patients in exercises and daily living activities, observe patients' progress, and report findings to your supervisor.

In order to help patients better understand their treatments, the reasons for these treatments, and the anticipated results, physical therapists, and in some cases their assistants, teach patients and their families about treatment. They also help patients and families understand the nature of home treatment.

As a physical therapist assistant, you can work in a variety of settings: hospitals, nursing homes, rehabilitation centers, school systems, and for home health agencies.

Some physical therapists have their own offices and employ assistants to help them. Others work in physicians' offices. Some specialize in pediatrics, geriatrics, orthopedics, sports medicine, neurology, or cardiopulmonary diseases.

Educational Paths

Physical therapist assistants must complete a two-year program, generally given at community or junior colleges. There are licensing requirements for physical therapist assistants in thirty-five states.

To further your career, you may want to become a physical therapist. To do so, you will have to (1) get a bachelor's degree in physical therapy, (2) join a certificate program that is for those who have taken bachelor's degrees in fields other than physical therapy, or (3) get a master's degree in physical therapy. You also must be licensed in all states to be a physical therapist.

Job Outlook

Jobs for physical therapist assistants are "expected to grow much faster than the average" predicts the *Occupational Outlook Handbook*. Growth is expected in the area of rehabilitation services for the disabled and the elderly. As these services continue to grow, so will the physical therapy field. There is presently and will continue to be an increase in the number of patients who need physical therapy services.

Professional Association

For more information, write to:

American Physical Therapy Association
1111 North Fairfax Street
Alexandria, VA 22314

Salary Information

According to a study of American Physical Therapy Association members, in 1986 physical therapist assistants made average salaries between $15,000 and $18,000, depending upon location.

Skills Needed by a Physical Therapist Assistant

Ability to:

1. Execute the physical therapist's plans and goals for patient treatment

2. Know human anatomy

3. Instruct patients

4. Help administer treatment using heat, massage, light, sound, and traction

5. Motivate

6. Be sensitive to patients

7. Be caring

8. Be patient

9. Help evaluate

10. Help others adapt

11. Work on a team

12. Stand for long periods on feet

13. Move equipment and help patients turn, stand, and walk

14. Appraise situations

15. Assess

16. Build confidence

17. Coach

18. Consult with physical therapist over patient's progress

19. Help make decisions based on treatment goals

20. Demonstrate

21. Encourage

22. Explain

23. Help patient improve

24. Observe

25. Persuade

26. Protect

Occupational Therapy Assistants: Teaching Others Life-Helping Skills

Do you want to work with the physically or mentally disabled? Do you want to be part of a health team and work under the supervision of an occupational therapist? Do you want to help provide activities and adaptive equipment to disabled patients? If you've answered yes, then you may want to join the rewarding profession of occupational therapy assistants (OTAs).

Under the supervision of an occupational therapist, you will help physically and mentally disabled patients become self-sufficient. You may teach a child a skill through games and toys or show older patients how to prepare meals, bathe, dress, and do other basic living skills. Through woodworking, leatherwork, or other therapeutic activities, you may help patients increase motor skills, strength, endurance, and concentration.

You may provide adaptive equipment for the disabled like wheelchairs, splints, and devices to help with eating and dressing. In groups or working alone with individuals, you will help your patients adjust to their disabilities. Time management, budgeting, shopping, meal preparation, homemaking, and self-care are some of the daily life activities you will teach.

Most occupational therapy assistants work with the physically handicapped; others work with the mentally disabled. You will

U.S. Department of Labor, Bureau of Labor Statistics, *Occupational Outlook Handbook*, 1982–1983.

probably work in a hospital, but some OTAs work for home health agencies, nursing homes, and school systems.

Educational Paths

Taking an educational program at a junior or community college is the best preparation for the field. Some people enter the field by taking a one-year program at a vocational or technical school. You'll study the physical sciences—anatomy and physiology—and occupational therapy theory and application. During your training, you will also be required to undergo at least two months of hands-on experience.

Those who graduate from approved programs and successfully complete a national examination are certified by the American Occupational Therapy Association to become a Certified Occupational Therapy Assistant (COTA). If you want to become an occupational therapist, additional training may not be necessary. After working for four years in an approved work setting and successfully completing an examination, you may be eligible for the designation of Registered Occupational Therapist (OTR).

Job Outlook

As with occupational therapists, "employment for occupational therapy assistants is expected to grow much faster than the average of all occupations throughout the 1990s because of increased growth or rehabilitation centers," says the *Occupational Outlook Handbook*. As the population lives longer, this older group, which tends to have more disabilities, will need the services of occupational therapy assistants. The outlook, in fact, is excellent for the field.

Professional Association

For more information, write to:

The American Occupational Therapy Association
1383 Piccard Drive
Rockland, MD 20850

Salary Information

According to a study by the Occupational Therapy Association, the average salary for an occupational therapy assistant was $16,200 in 1986.

Skills Needed by an Occupational Therapy Assistant

Ability to:

1. Work with the disabled
2. Teach
3. Motivate
4. Plan programs
5. Follow through
6. Maintain equipment and tools
7. Create
8. Work well under pressure
9. Work with others on a team
10. Help rehabilitate
11. Work under supervision
12. Get along with the public

13. Care for others

14. Keep records

15. Comfort patients

16. Counsel

17. Make decisions

18. Evaluate

19. Explain treatment plans to patients and families

20. Initiate

21. Listen

22. Work with a group

23. Monitor patients' progress with help of occupational therapist

24. Observe

25. Persuade

Dental Assistants: Chairside Assistants

Walk into any dentist's office, and you will be escorted to the treatment room. Awaiting you will be the dental assistant, who will make you comfortable, prepare you for your treatment, and locate your dental records. Once the dentist appears, the dental assistant assists the dentist by arranging the proper treatment instruments on a tray. Once work begins, she hands the dentist the proper materials for fillings, extractions, root canal work, and so on; takes x-rays; and makes sure that your mouth is clear by using a suction device. If surgery is required, she will provide post-

---

U.S. Department of Labor, Bureau of Labor Statistics, *Occupational Outlook Handbook*, 1986.

operative instruction. And for all patients, she'll give instructions on dental and oral health practices.

As a dental assistant, you will be responsible for many duties: office, laboratory, and clinical work; preparation of materials for making impressions and restorations; taking x-rays of patients' teeth and processing the film; sterilization and disinfection of instruments and equipment; and in some states, the application of medications to the teeth and tissue. If you work in a small office, you may be responsible for its management: making appointments, sending out and collecting bills, processing insurance forms, meeting with sales representatives from dental-product manufacturers, and so forth. In larger offices, you may be responsible only for dental assistant duties.

Dental assisting is a field open to high school graduates. It is an exciting entry-level job that offers many opportunities to move up the dental field's hierarchy. Some dental assistants eventually become dental hygienists.

Educational Paths

Many dental assistants learn their work on-the-job. Basic job requirements are a pleasing personality and the willingness and ability to learn the job. Some dental assistants, however, complete dental-assisting programs at junior community colleges, trade schools, or technical institutes. Most programs are for one year only, but taking a two-year program at community or junior colleges can lead to an associate degree. The key admissions requirement to these programs is a high school diploma, but some require typing or a science course.

Although there are some four- or six-month programs offered by private vocational schools, they aren't approved or accredited by the dental profession.

If you are already a dental assistant, there is a correspondence course given by the University of North Carolina School of Dentistry that is accredited by the Commission of Dental Accreditation. It is for those employed dental assistants who can't participate in a full-time program and is a good way to learn the academics of the field.

Job Outlook

Employment prospects for dental assistants are expected to grow faster than average throughout the 1990s predicts the *Occupational Outlook Handbook*. As the dental field expands and improves, there is a continuing need for trained dental workers.

Professional Associations

For more information, write to:

American Dental Assistants Association
666 North Lake Shore Drive, Suite 1130
Chicago, IL 60611

National Association of Dental Assistants
900 South Washington Street, Suite G13
Falls Church, VA 22046

Salary Information

As a dental assistant, your salary will depend on many factors: duties, responsibilities, geographic location, and employer's policy concerning pay.

According to the National Association of Dental Assistants, a salary survey of its members revealed that most dental assistants had gross annual incomes over $16,000; the overall average annual salary was $14,800 in 1986.

Skills Needed by a Dental Assistant

Ability to:

1. Work under the supervision of a dentist

2. Meet the public

3. Learn and know dental instruments and equipment

4. Use dental x-ray equipment and process film

5. Prepare dental materials

6. File and retrieve dental records

7. Use dental suction equipment

8. Make impressions

9. Sterilize instruments

10. Put patients at ease

11. Work for long periods on feet

12. Use manual dexterity

13. Do billing procedures

14. Process dental insurance claims

15. Order dental products and deal with dental-product man-ufacturing reps

16. Advise patients on proper oral health practices

17. Give postoperative instructions to patients

18. Manage dental office

19. Obtain information from patients

20. Maintain a congenial personality

Dispensing Opticians: Lens Workers

If you wear glasses or contact lenses, you've probably used the services of the dispensing optician. Unlike the ophthalmologist, who is a medical doctor who diagnoses eye diseases and who can surgically correct eye problems or prescribe drugs, and unlike the optometrist who examines patients' eyes and can write prescriptions for eye problem correction, the optician dispenses the lenses. In order to do this, she follows the prescriptions given by the ophthalmologist or optometrist.

A dispensing optician can help you select eyeglass frames and adjust finished frames. This eye professional usually measures the distance between a customer's eyes to determine the best placement of lenses. Then she looks at the customer's hairstyle and facial features to determine the best type of frame.

After the customer has chosen a frame she prepares an order for the ophthalmology laboratory so that the lenses can be ground and inserted into a frame. But an optician may do her own ophthalmic laboratory work. Once the lenses are completed, the optician adjusts the frame to fit the customer's bone structure of the face and head. She also checks for sturdiness of the lenses.

As a dispensing optician, you can also fit contact lenses in states that approve that procedure. You will follow the ophthalmologist's or optometrist's prescription and measure the corneas of the customer's eyes. After the lenses are ready, you show customers how to insert and take care of the lenses.

As a dispensing optician, you will primarily work for retail eyeglass stores. You can work in your own business or work for an established optician or optometrist.

Educational Paths

If you're a high school graduate, you can learn to be a dispensing optician on-the-job. This on-the-job training can last for several years, depending on the employer. Increasingly, those with some training in the field have a competitive edge.

You can take opticianry training at community colleges, vocational or technical institutes, trade schools, and manufacturers training programs. There are associate degree programs in the field, and some are accredited by the Commission on Opticianry Accreditation. There are also short, six-month to one-year programs that can lead to certification.

Some optical dispensing companies offer two- to four-year apprenticeship programs. You'll receive training in optical mathematics, optical physics, and the use of laboratory equipment. You'll get technical training and learn office management and sales.

In twenty states and Puerto Rico, dispensing opticians' credentials are obtained through licensing or voluntary certification or registration.

Job Outlook

Employment is expected "to increase about as fast as the average for all occupations through the mid-1990s." A need for corrective lenses and the public's awareness of the importance of good eye care are contributory factors.

Professional Association

For more information, write to:

Opticians Association of America
10341 Democracy Lane
P.O. Box 10110
Fairfax, VA 22030

Salary Information

Starting salaries for licensed, dispensing opticians in the New York City area were between $300 and $360 a week in 1985. On the average, experienced opticians in New York City made at least $400 a week. Those dispensing opticians who own their own businesses made $30,000 or more a year.

Skills Needed by an Optician

Ability to:

1. Know field of opticianry
2. Take and place orders
3. Do paperwork
4. Do detail work
5. Deal with public
6. Measure
7. Help others select glasses
8. Understand facial and head structures in relation to frames
9. Check for quality
10. Make adjustments
11. Use tools: optical pliers, files, and screwdrivers
12. Prepare specifications
13. Fit contact lenses (permitted in some states)
14. Be patient
15. Stand and work on feet for long periods of time
16. Assess
17. Calculate costs

18. Cooperate with others

19. Be pleasant

20. Discuss options

21. Dispense

22. Evaluate

23. Follow through

24. Perform with manual dexterity

25. Organize

26. Solve problems

27. Recommend

28. Keep records

29. Do technical work

30. Work with precision

Emergency Medical Technicians: Dealing with Emergencies

An elderly man has collapsed in a shopping mall. An SOS is sounded and the emergency medical technicians (EMTs) jump into the ambulance and zoom to the scene. At the mall, the EMTs begin trying to revive him. For half an hour they work on the man, who eventually gains consciousness. He is taken by ambulance to the hospital. The emergency medical technician team has just saved another life.

A suburban housewife has fallen off a ladder and her back is aching. Her children call 911 (the emergency number in many

U.S. Department of Labor, Bureau of Labor Statistics, *Occupational Outlook Handbook*, 1986.

states), and the emergency medical technicians are summoned. After arriving at the house, they carefully examine the woman and place a splint on her back. She is carefully placed on a stretcher and wheeled into the ambulance and taken to a hospital.

Emergency medical technicians help people in emergency situations and save lives. They help accident and heart attack victims and others who need emergency help. As an EMT, you will work for the fire or police departments, private ambulance companies, or hospitals. Your work will be stressful, demanding, challenging, and full of life-and-death drama. You will be part of the health team that daily saves the lives of hundreds of emergency victims.

Although it is currently a male-dominated field, the *Journal of Emergency Medical Services* reports that 6 percent of the total number of EMTs are women, with 19 percent of the private EMTs and 28 percent of the hospital-based EMTs being female.

Educational Paths

To become an emergency medical technician, you must take a formal training course, be at least 18 years of age, have a high school diploma or equivalent, and have a valid driver's license. If you have taken health and science courses in high school, you have some preparation for the field. Armed Forces training as a medic is also good preparation.

The formal training course is the standard 110-hour program that was designed by the U.S. Department of Transportation. Police, fire, and health departments offer the course. Medical schools, colleges, and universities also offer it as a nondegree course.

Job Outlook

The U.S. Department of Labor, Bureau of Labor Statistics, expects employment for EMTs to "grow more slowly than the average for all occupations." Conflicting forces will share the job outlook. On the one hand, population growth and especially an increase in the number of older people are expected to spur demand for EMTs. Other factors are likely to constrict job growth, however. Of foremost importance is the rising cost of training and equipping EMTs.

Professional Association

For more career and educational information, write to:

The National Association of
Emergency Medical Technicians
P.O. Box 334
Newton Highlands, MA 02161

Salary Information

Factors such as geographic location of job, training, and experience affect salaries for emergency medical technicians. A 1987 survey by the *Journal of Emergency Medical Services* concluded that the average annual salary for full-time EMT-ambulance workers was $18,700; EMT-intermediates made average annual salaries of $18,800 and EMT-paramedics made $24,300.

Skills Needed by an Emergency Medical Technician

Ability to:

1. Deal with emergencies

2. Deal with stressful situations

3. Use machines that save lives

4. Analyze situations

5. Care for others

6. Communicate orally

7. Help victims relax

8. Examine

9. Get cooperation from others

10. Diagnose

11. Evaluate

12. Follow through

13. Deal with the public

14. Deal with death and dying

15. Locate

16. Observe

17. Obtain information

18. Keep records of emergencies

19. Recognize problems

20. Make recommendations

21. Work on a team

22. Understand

23. Work with others at the scene of an emergency

24. Coordinate

25. Help lift up to 100 pounds

11

Creative Careers

Commercial and Graphic Designers: Drawing Up Commercials

A large car company needs an advertisement and calls XYZ Advertising Agency for assistance. The agency's account executive assesses the client's needs, and a creative plan is devised. The account executive, art director, and copywriter begin brainstorming until a satisfactory creative plan is developed. The agency's creative director critiques it and accepts or rejects it. A presentation is prepared, and the account executive shows it to the client. If the client approves, the creative wheels are set in action.

The art director, who is in charge of the art, design, photography, and style of the published materials and TV advertisements, selects the best artist to do the advertisement's illustration. The commercial artist may be on the agency's staff, or she may be a free-lancer, who will be contracted to do this particular job.

U.S. Department of Labor, Bureau of Labor Statistics, *Occupational Outlook Handbook*, 1986.

Most commercial artists are full-timers. Most start as paste-up or layout assistants. They work for advertising agencies; publishing houses; magazines and newspapers; local, state, and federal government agencies; graphic art studios; department stores; manufacturing firms; and so on. A good number are self-employed and work as free-lancers. Many tend to work in large cities like New York, Chicago, and Los Angeles, where advertising and publishing flourish.

Educational Paths

Talent and ability are the most important qualities needed for work as a commercial and graphic artist. A portfolio with your best work is the selling card in the profession; it's the "résumé" that opens doors.

Many artists are self-taught, but increasingly many are becoming trained in art schools, junior or community colleges, universities, or technical schools. Although talent is still a requirement, getting some formal training that will develop technical skills will give you the competitive edge.

Job Outlook

Many people are attracted to this field because it is a glamorous and exciting area. This makes the field very competitive. However, the *Occupational Outlook Handbook* predicts that employment for commercial and graphic artists is "expected to grow faster than average for all occupations through the 1990s." But talented individuals with business savvy and contacts will have the most opportunities.

Professional Association

For more information, write to:

Graphic Artists Guild
11 West 20th Street
New York, NY 10011

Salary Information

Median annual salaries for graphic artists (full-time) were approximately $20,000 in 1986. According to the U.S. Department of Labor's *Occupational Outlook Handbook*, the middle 50 percent of graphic artists made between $15,200 and $26,000.

Skills Needed by a Commercial or Graphic Artist

Ability to:

1. Be creative

2. Compile a good portfolio

3. Have flair and style

4. Conceptualize

5. Visualize

6. Appraise

7. Calculate costs of projects (if working free-lance)

8. Coordinate

9. Create

10. Deal with pressure

11. Meet deadlines

12. Make decisions

13. Design

14. Endure long hours of work

15. Evaluate

16. Explain

17. Handle criticism

18. Imagine

19. Initiate

20. Listen

21. Make layouts

22. Negotiate contracts

23. Obtain information

24. Organize

25. Persuade

26. Work on a team

27. Work alone

28. Follow through

Photographers: Snap This Up

A picture, they say, is worth a thousand words. Getting paid for that picture is the photographer's business. Photographers get paid to snap newsworthy stories, fashion models, babies, actors, products, food and industrial scenes, and so forth. For these services, some of them are very handsomely paid.

There are several types of photographers: motion picture, scientific, biologic, and industrial photographers and photojournalists, to name a few. But you are probably most familiar with still photographers and photojournalists. Still photographers capture images of individuals and groups at events like weddings or christenings. Some just capture the nuances of life and make books of their pictures. On the other hand, photojournalists concentrate on the newsworthy, and their work appears in magazines, newspapers, or on television news shows. Industrial photographers focus on photos with an industrial slant. They may do catalog photographs or snap company employees for a house organ or newsletter or take a photograph of a worker standing beside new equipment.

Motion picture photographers specialize in a field like medicine, science, news, or fashion and advertising.

Scientific and biologic photographers concentrate on photographs and slides for scientific reports and publications. Some specialize in engineering, aerodynamics, medicine, biology, or chemistry.

Commercial photographers work in the glamour fields of fashion and advertising. Many are free-lancers who sell their works to magazines and advertising agencies. Although competitive, these areas produce hefty paychecks for photographers.

Educational Paths

There are no formal educational requirements for the field: some photographers haven't finished high school; some are high school graduates; others have finished two- or four-year colleges.

Although you can learn photography in vocational or art schools, junior or community colleges and universities, many photographers learn the trade in two or three years of on-the-job training as photographers' assistants at commercial studios. Most trainees start in the darkroom and learn chemical mixing, film developing, photoprinting, and enlarging. Some go to work for newspapers or other companies or work as apprentices for free-lance photographers.

Regardless of how you prepare for the field, talent, technical understanding of photography, creativity, imagination, and timing are the best qualifications for a photographer.

Job Outlook

The *Occupational Outlook Handbook* says employment for photographers and camera operators is expected to grow faster than the average for all occupations through the mid-1990s.

Professional Association

For more information, write to:

Professional Photographers of America, Inc.
1090 Executive Way
Des Plaines, IL 60018

Salary Information

From a survey of its members, the American Society of Magazine Photographers reports that full-time photographers made mean net incomes of $36,800 in 1985; 25 percent made between $10,000 and $25,000; 30 percent made between $25,000 and $50,000. The highest-paid group worked in the advertising and fashion fields and averaged about $45,000. The lowest-paid group worked in editorial and public relations fields and earned between $26,000 and $30,000.

Skills Needed by a Photographer

Ability to:

1. Capture personalities or moods
2. Skillfully use a camera
3. Develop different varieties of film
4. Use lenses for the right effect
5. Mix chemicals
6. Do photoprinting and enlarging
7. Carry heavy equipment
8. Be imaginative
9. Be original
10. Write (if working as a photojournalist)
11. Get people to relax
12. Assess needs of clients
13. Appraise situations and people
14. Do bookkeeping
15. Budget
16. Catalog
17. Classify
18. Communicate
19. Make decisions
20. Direct others
21. Evaluate
22. Exhibit
23. Experiment

24. Follow through
25. Improve
26. Inspire
27. Judge
28. Meet the public
29. Observe
30. Persuade
31. Make recommendations to clients
32. Make schedules
33. Visualize
34. Work with others

A Photographer Must Also Have the Following Qualities:

1. Good vision
2. Artistic ability
3. Manual dexterity

12

Legal Careers

Legal Assistants: Lawyers' Helpers

One of the twenty fastest growing occupations is that of the legal assistant, or the paralegal profession. Opportunities are plentiful for these workers, who first emerged in the late 1960s.

As a legal assistant, you will do the background work for an attorney. Your duties will include helping your boss prepare for trials by investigating facts of cases and researching and identifying appropriate laws, judicial decisions, legal articles, or other relevant materials. After your preliminary research, you will prepare written reports to help the attorney assess the case. If she or he decides to take the case and bring a lawsuit, you may prepare legal arguments and other documents needed for the case.

Legal assistants work for private attorneys; small, medium, and large law firms; community legal service agencies; government agencies; banks; insurance companies; or corporations. You may specialize in one type of law such as family law, real estate, estate

U.S. Department of Labor, Bureau of Labor Statistics, *Occupational Outlook Handbook*, 1986.

planning, labor law, litigation, or corporate law. And the nature of your duties will depend upon where you work. For example, a legal assistant working for a small law firm or a single attorney may be required to handle more responsibilities than one working for a larger firm.

If you choose to look for employment at a small law firm, you will have the best employment prospects. And working for community legal services may also offer good employment opportunities.

Educational Paths

Some employers will train high school graduates for legal assistant positions. However, an increasing number of employers want employees to have some formal training. This training can be taken at business or vocational schools, community and junior colleges, paralegal institutes, universities, and so on. Admissions requirements for these programs may vary. Some schools require that candidates have some college courses or even a college degree; others accept high school graduates and/or those with legal experience.

Most programs are for two years, but some take a few months or as long as four years. Pay particular attention to the type of program you take. To determine the best program for you, do some research. Some are accredited by the American Bar Association; others aren't. Check with several law firms, private attorneys, and corporations to determine educational and work requirements for your area.

In order to progress in your career, you may want to get certification from the National Association of Legal Assistants. Although this certification is voluntary, it is a mark of achievement in the field. If you decide to become certified, you must meet various standards including educational and work experience and the successful passing of a two-day examination given by the Certifying Board of Legal Assistants. If you meet these requirements, you will be eligible for designation of Certified Legal Assistant (CLA).

Job Outlook

The U.S. Department of Labor, Bureau of Labor Statistics, says that employment opportunities for legal assistants will "increase significantly through the mid-1990s." Competition will be keen for these jobs because of the increasing interest in the field and the large number of graduates from legal assistant programs.

Professional Associations

For more information, write to:

National Association of Legal
    Assistants, Inc.
1420 South Utica
Tulsa, OK 74104

For career information and a list of accredited programs, write to:

American Bar Association
Standing Committee on Legal Assistants
750 North Lake Shore Drive
Chicago, IL 60611

Salary Information

Salaries for legal assistants vary according to several factors: training, experience, and geographic location of job. Those in large metropolitan areas earn the most.

Skills Needed by a Legal Assistant

Ability to:

1. Assist attorneys
2. Think logically
3. Communicate both orally and in writing
4. Take direction
5. Understand legal terminology
6. Do research
7. Do investigations
8. Interview and extract information from clients
9. Operate and apply computers in legal research
10. Stay abreast of changes in law field
11. Keep information confidential
12. Be courteous
13. Deal with the public
14. Be ethical
15. Follow through
16. Get the job done
17. Analyze
18. Make decisions
19. Prepare documents
20. Review materials
21. Work long hours in law library
22. Do detail work

Court Reporters: $40,000–$50,000 Recorders

Enter the world of court reporting and find yourself in the throes of courtroom drama. Court reporters are familiar to us because we have repeatedly seen them in courtroom scenes in our favorite television movies and films. The court reporter is the one the whole court looks at when the judge instructs her to "strike that from the record." She is the observant recorder of legal proceedings who uses the stenotype machine or Steno Mask (an audio typing machine) and ultimately makes sure there is an official record or transcript. For these services, she is handsomely paid. In some cities, for example, beginners start at $25,000, and those with a few years' experience make between $40,000 and $50,000.

Some court reporters are salaried; others free-lance or own businesses. They work for courts, governmental agencies, attorneys, or companies that need proceedings or conferences recorded. For the free-lancer or business owner, this field offers flexible hours and travel opportunities.

As a court reporter, you must be able to sit for long periods of time, be able to concentrate and be observant, and be able to understand and record legal terminology. You must be a top-notch follow-through person who can meet deadlines and work under pressure. This is a demanding career, and you must be able to meet the challenges of the job. If you have the necessary qualities and skills, you can make it in this exciting field.

Educational Paths

Training for court reporters usually takes place in business schools, in junior or community colleges, or on-the-job. Generally, you should take a two-year program with courses in legal and medical

---

U.S. Department of Labor, Bureau of Labor Statistics, *Occupational Outlook Handbook*, 1986.

terminology, speed building, business law, business English, and multivoice transcription. Although some programs last two years, others permit students to work at their own pace.

According to the Association of Independent Colleges and Universities, general skills for court reporters would be "225 WPM accurate typing speed on the stenotype machine, skill for recording two, three, and four way conversations, expert knowledge of specialized terminology for legal, medical and insurance work, and familiarity with legal and medical procedures."

In some states, you must be licensed, and a license is obtained by taking an examination. The National Shorthand Reporters Association also gives the designation of registered professional reporter (RPR), for those who have passed a two-part examination and have continuing education credits. If you get the RPR, you'll be recognized for excellence in the field.

Job Outlook

The *Occupational Outlook Handbook* says the demand for skilled shorthand or court reporters should remain strong.

Professional Association

For more information, write to:

National Shorthand Reporters Association
118 Park Street, SE
Vienna, VA 22180

Salary Information

The *Occupational Outlook Handbook* reports that court reporters (legal stenographers) in the private sector earned average salaries of $17,056 in 1985. But according to the Stenotype Institute, court reporters in New York, for example, start at salaries of $25,000; those with a few years' experience make between $40,000 and $50,000 a year.

Skills Needed by a Court Reporter

Ability to:

1. Take transcription on stenotype machine at 225 WPM
2. Take audio transcription on Steno Mask machine
3. Learn and know legal and medical terminology
4. Do multivoice transcription
5. Spell, punctuate, and use vocabulary skills
6. Work on a team
7. Have a good appearance
8. Sit for long periods of time
9. Observe
10. Be impartial
11. Follow through
12. Work under pressure
13. Meet deadlines
14. Be thorough
15. Listen
16. Manage time
17. Be prompt
18. Concentrate
19. Operate a business
20. Free-lance

13

Travel Careers

Travel Agents: Plotters of Unforgettable Trips

Mary Jones and Karl Kramer are planning the perfect honeymoon. Linda Kellogs wants to take her elderly mother on a trip around the world. Carolyn Hilton wants to meet single men at a singles' resort. Polly Anderson does frequent business traveling and wants the best airline rates. What do these five people have in common? All need and should use the services of a travel agent.

Travel agents provide travel counseling, help you select the perfect trip, can save you a bundle on discount fares and group trips, and/or make sure that you enjoy or are satisfied with your trip. They are the patient souls who pore over travel brochures or other travel material to help ensure your perfect trip. They must size up your situation and accommodate your specific needs and pocketbook by using their experience and knowledge to provide you with the best.

A good agent can be worth hundreds or even thousands to her

U.S. Department of Labor, Bureau of Labor Statistics, *Occupational Outlook Handbook*, 1986.

clients. She can help make your trip enjoyable or a disaster. For example, an agent who finds a vacation spot for a couple with two children must consider the children's needs in the vacation planning. If she locates a vacation resort that has activities for children, she'll ensure the couple's enjoyment of the trip. On the other hand, if she sends two single women to a hotel that's occupied by mostly married couples, her clients probably won't enjoy themselves.

Since travel agents are paid by commission, the best way for them to get high financial rewards is to please their customers. A good, thorough travel agent will have clients clamoring for more.

Educational Paths

Many travel agents learn on-the-job in company-sponsored training programs or in travel courses at vocational schools, adult educational programs, junior or community colleges, or certificate programs at colleges and universities. If you've had courses in history, geography, foreign languages, or data processing, you have a good background for the travel agent business. Or if you have traveled to many countries and experienced many cultures, you can be an asset to the industry.

As you gain experience, you may want to take an advanced course that will make you eligible for certification by the Institute of Certified Travel Agents. Or you may want to get a certificate of proficiency from the American Society of Travel Agents, by successfully passing a test about travel agents' duties.

Job Outlook

Employment of travel agents is expected to grow faster than the average for all occupations. Although the travel industry is usually dependent on the economy, things look very promising throughout the 1990s.

Professional Association

For career and training information, write to:

American Society of Travel Agents
11 King Street
Alexandria, VA 22314

Salary Information

Salaries for travel agents depend on several factors: experience, size and location of work site, and sales ability. The American Society of Travel Agents reports that their 1987 salary survey revealed that the average weekly salary for entry-level travel agents was $229; for those with one year's experience it was $279; three years' experience, $303; five years' experience, $368; ten years' experience, $400. Managers made weekly salaries of $578.

Skills Needed by a Travel Agent

Ability to:

1. Have patience

2. Counsel others

3. Make arrangements

4. Promote

5. Confer with others

6. Do detail work

7. Type

8. Follow through

9. Be client's advocate

10. Appraise situations

11. Calculate

12. Brainstorm

13. Communicate orally and in writing

14. Persuade

15. Compare

16. Analyze situations

17. Critique

18. Consult

19. Cooperate

20. Compute

21. Develop

22. Discuss

23. Encourage

24. Estimate

25. Evaluate

26. Explain

27. File

28. Gather information

29. Handle complaints

30. Initiate

31. Teach

32. Investigate

33. Listen

34. Locate

35. Deal with the public

36. Motivate

37. Observe

38. Organize

39. Be orderly

40. Perform well under stress

41. Persevere

42. Plan

43. Process

44. Recognize problems

45. Make recommendations

46. Keep records

47. Reduce costs

48. Represent agency to the public

49. Review

50. Stimulate

51. Determine strategy

14

Sales Careers

Insurance Agents and Brokers:
Making It in a Premium Career

Do you want to double your current salary and make $35,000, $50,000, or more a year? If so, try a premium insurance career.

Many of you may be leery of an insurance career and say, "Thank you, but no thank you." Insurance careers may conjure up visions of agents pounding the pavement, desperately trying to convince consumers to get adequate protection. You don't want to deal with a career focusing on death. Wrong! Insurance is so much more than death benefits.

Without insurance, our cost of living would skyrocket. Can you imagine paying the entire cost of a two-week hospital stay without insurance? With escalating hospital costs, you could be wiped out financially. What about those with catastrophic illnesses, who would go bankrupt without insurance?

Or in the event of fire or natural disaster, could you refurnish

---

U.S. Department of Labor, Bureau of Labor Statistics, *Occupational Outlook Handbook*, 1986.

your home or apartment without the help of insurance coverage? Own a business? What would happen if your inventory was completely destroyed by fire or vandalism?

What if your car were destroyed in an accident? Would you have the money to replace it? Or what if someone were killed in an accident involving your car? Could you compensate the victim's family? Insurance affects all of our lives. Without it, we would have to deplete our finances to cover our losses.

As a career, work as an insurance agent offers many flexibilities that working women need: flexible hours, salaries based on your performance (commissions), and so on. It is a career that has traditionally welcomed high school graduates, and it is a field open to career changers. It is also a field in which you have an opportunity to be self-employed.

Both insurance agents and brokers work in the insurance field. Insurance agents work for specific companies; brokers are independent professionals who sell policies for several companies and select the best one for their clients.

Agents and brokers can sell one or more types of insurance: life, property-liability (casualty), and health. Those who specialize in life insurance sell policies that give protection for funeral expenses and provide financial support for survivors. But life insurance policies are so much more and can be used for retirement, children's education, and other things while customers are living.

Casualty insurance agents help clients protect against losses from automobile accidents, fire or theft, and other misfortunes. Some casualty agents help clients with worker's compensation, product liability, and/or malpractice.

Both life and casualty agents sell insurance that helps defer hospital costs or provide coverage for loss of income from illness (disability insurance).

Educational Paths

An increasing number of insurance companies may *prefer* college graduates, but most still hire high school graduates. By showing the potential to sell or having prior sales ability, you can qualify for an insurance agent's position.

All insurance agents or brokers must be licensed by your state. In order to be licensed, you must pass a written examination. You can prepare for the test with company training. Most insurance companies provide some training, other companies have pretest courses to help agents prepare for the exam.

To really advance in the field, you need additional training. You can specialize in insurance at four-year colleges and universities, like the College of Insurance in New York. Some insurance workers who want to advance in their careers get industry designations. One such designation is awarded by the Life Underwriter Training Council (LUTC), which gives a certificate in life insurance marketing. Courses in this two-year program stress selling; other courses are in health insurance and advanced sales techniques. Another designation is the Registered Health Underwriter (RHU), available from the National Association of Health Underwriters for those who successfully complete their courses.

Agents and brokers can get the Chartered Life Underwriter (CLU) designation to advance their career. Or there is the Chartered Financial Consultant (ChFC) from the College of Certified Planning for those interested in financial planning. To get the ChFC designation, you must know tax laws, estate planning, investments, and other financial planning matters. You can qualify for both the CLU and the ChFC by successfully passing a series of examinations given by the American College, Bryn Mawr, Pennsylvania.

If you want to work as a property casualty agent, you will want to get the Chartered Property Casualty Underwriter (CPCU) designation for maximum career advancement. You can receive this designation by passing examinations given by the American Institute for Property and Liability Underwriters.

You can get another industry designation: Accredited Advisor in

Insurance. As an agent or broker, you can take courses in insurance production, multiple-lines insurance protection, and agency operation and marketing to qualify.

Job Outlook

The *Occupational Outlook Handbook* says employment for insurance agents and brokers is "best for ambitious people who enjoy sales work and who are able to develop expertise in a wide range of insurance and financial services."

Professional Associations

For more information, write to:

American Council of Life Insurance
1000 Pennsylvania Avenue, NW
Washington, D.C. 20004

National Association of Insurance Women
P.O. Box 4410
Tulsa, OK 74159

In addition, minority women can write to:

National Insurance Association
2400 South Michigan Avenue
Chicago, IL 60616
(for information on membership only)

Salary Information

Salaries for beginning insurance agents who worked for large companies were $1,400 a month in 1986. Life insurance workers with five to ten years' experience made median salaries of approximately

$47,000 a year in 1986; those with about ten years' or more experience made median salaries of $70,000. One in every five workers in the field made more than $100,000 a year.

Skills Needed by an Insurance Agent or Broker

Ability to:

1. Sell
2. Help others select best policies
3. Persuade
4. Motivate
5. Help others plan for the future
6. Locate the best company with best policy for customers
7. Work independently
8. Do detail work
9. Travel to customers
10. Learn insurance laws
11. Pass examinations needed for licensing
12. Deal with the public
13. Produce
14. Advise
15. Analyze
16. Approve
17. Assess
18. Calculate costs

19. Communicate

20. Consult

21. Counsel

22. Educate public

23. Follow through

24. Initiate

25. Interview

26. Listen

27. Manage accounts

28. Observe

29. Obtain information

30. Persuade

31. Plan

32. Present policies and discuss options

33. Promote

34. Speak in front of groups

35. Recognize problems

36. Run one's own business

37. Research

38. Review

39. Motivate oneself

40. Schedule appointments

41. Solve problems

42. Summarize

43. Work on a team

44. Work with others

Real Estate Agents and Brokers: Sellers of the Land

Today's booming real estate field offers many opportunities for its specialists. Some of those who are the recipients of the industry's boom are its salespeople: real estate agents and brokers.

As a real estate agent or broker, you may sell your communities' hottest real estate properties. As your client's advocate, you may specialize in residential sales or the selling of homes. Or you may be a commercial agent or broker, selling commercial real estate property like office space or apartment buildings. Or you may be in real estate syndication and put together a number of investors to purchase large properties. Or perhaps the area of land development is intriguing to you.

The entire real estate field offers exciting opportunities to those who know where they are going and work hard to succeed, because much of your success in the field is determined by your own initiative. So this is a career for those who are aggressive in terms of creating opportunities for themselves as well as establishing a solid client base. And it is a field for those who believe in themselves and are willing to do the research and hard work.

Real estate is a great field, especially for the woman without a degree and particularly for the career changer or housewife returning to the job market. It is a field that offers flexible hours, even part-time work.

U.S. Department of Labor, Bureau of Labor Statistics, *Occupational Outlook Handbook*, 1986.

Educational Paths

Most real estate people start as agents, then become brokers. In order to become an agent, you must be licensed in every state and the District of Columbia. State licensing requirements include being a high school graduate and at least 18 years of age and passing a written examination. In order to qualify for the general sales license, you should have at least 30 hours of classroom instruction, which can be taken at junior or community colleges, four-year colleges or universities, adult education programs, or through local boards that are members of the National Association of Realtors.

After you have your real estate license, you will probably work in residential sales. But after you have established yourself, you may become a broker—an independent businessperson who has the ability to close real estate deals. In order to become a broker, you must also be licensed by your state; licensing requirements include having at least one to three years of selling experience and at least 90 hours of formal training and successfully passing a written examination.

After you have been in the field for a while, you may want to specialize in one of real estate's specialties: commercial brokerage, real estate appraising, property management, land development, urban planning, real estate securities and syndication, real estate counseling, and real estate research (see Figure 22).

FIGURE 22
Real Estate Specialties

Residential Brokerage

Largest single field of real estate activity

- Good opportunities for rapid advancement and increasing income
- Requires broad knowledge of community and neighborhoods, economics, real estate law, finance, and the money market

Commercial Brokerage

Specializing in income-producing properties (for example, apartment and office buildings, retail stores, warehouses)

Industrial Brokerage

Developing, selling, or leasing properties for industry or manufacturing

Farm and Land Brokerage

Not necessarily limited to farmland. Cities often require rural land for expansion; farm management for absentee owners also a possibility

- On-the-job training a must; formal agricultural training an advantage

Real Estate Appraising

Gathering and evaluating all facts affecting property's value and rendering an opinion of that value

- Many different types—assessed value, insured value, loan value, market value
- Some appraising knowledge required for any real estate work

Property Management

Supervising every aspect of the property's operation to produce the highest possible financial return over the longest period of time

- Includes renting, tenant relations, building maintenance and repair, supervising personnel and tradesmen, accounting, and advertising

Land Development

Turning raw land into marketable, profitable subdivisions, shopping centers, industrial parks, and so on

- Includes selecting sites, analyzing costs, securing financing, contracting for physical buildings, supervising construction, and promoting finished development to prospects

Urban Planning

Anticipating city's future growth, and proposing productive, economical ways of using land and water resources to accommodate this growth

Real Estate Securities and Syndication

Developing and offering limited partnership in real estate for investment purposes

- Generates capital for expanding the real estate industry
- Gives individuals the opportunity to invest in large properties without becoming involved in management or exposed to unlimited liability

Real Estate Counseling

Giving advice about property, frequently on productive uses for different kinds, or income opportunities

Real Estate Research

Providing precise information on land use, urban environmental patterns, and market trends

- Physical—finding ways to improve buildings
- Economic—compiling data for future planning—probable demand for new homes, percentage of substandard housing, changes in financing and interest rates, effects of urban planning programs, and so on.

Source: *Careers in Real Estate*, National Association of Realtors, 1975.

Job Outlook

The *Occupational Outlook Handbook* predicts that real estate employment "is expected to grow about as fast as the average for all occupations through the mid-1990s in order to satisfy the demand for housing and other properties."

Professional Associations

For more information, write to:

National Association of Realtors
430 North Michigan Avenue
Chicago, IL 60611

In addition, minority women can write to:

National Association of Real Estate Brokers
1101 14th Street, NW
Suite 1000
Washington, D.C. 20005

Salary Information

Most agents work on commission and share it with their brokers after properties are sold. According to the National Association of Realtors' membership profile of 1987, the median annual income for brokers was $35,000 in 1986; the median annual income for salespeople was $19,400.

Skills Needed by a Real Estate Agent or Broker

Ability to:

1. Sell
2. Deal with the public
3. Be enthusiastic about work and sales properties
4. Be honest
5. Have a good appearance
6. Use computers
7. Work independently
8. Persuade
9. Work with people
10. Follow through
11. Negotiate
12. Close deals
13. Promote one's business and oneself
14. Advise
15. Calculate costs
16. Appraise
17. Outline costs of projects
18. Communicate both orally and in writing
19. Appraise situations
20. Be advocate for clients
21. Deal with pressure
22. Make decisions

23. Work long hours

24. Explain

25. Handle complaints

26. Investigate

27. Find or locate property

28. Initiate

29. Inspect properties

30. Listen

31. Manage work of others

32. Motivate others

33. Organize

34. Observe

35. Obtain information

36. Administrate well

Manufacturer's Salespeople: Selling Goods

Many women have misconceptions about the sales field. In order to be successful in sales, they feel it requires aggressive, pushy, and greedy attitudes. But nothing could be further from the truth. Salespeople aren't like the 1950s television characterizations of the pushy salesman. They are professional workers who do their bidding without pushing their products down their clients' throats. In fact, most are more persuasive than pushy.

Salespeople are usually initiators, whose salaries match their ef-

---

U.S. Department of Labor, Bureau of Labor Statistics, *Occupational Outlook Handbook*, 1986.

forts. Good salespeople, therefore, make top dollar. Some make more than $50,000 a year.

Where do manufacturer's salespeople work? They work for a wide variety of manufacturers in the food, chemical, beauty supply, computer, or other fields. Most of them are responsible for large territories and are generally on the go. Their paperwork is done at the manufacturer's office or plant, and their selling is done "in the field" visiting their clients. As a result, salespeople are rarely desk-bound, but rather active go-getters.

The salesperson's main task is to convince buyers to purchase her company's products. She can achieve this by sizing up her customers' needs and making product suggestions. Or she can recommend new products that will improve her customers' efficiency.

If you work as a manufacturer's salesperson, you will be working in a stepping-stone position that can lead to management opportunities. In fact, many top executives, including many chief executive officers, began their careers in sales. It is a position that enables you to learn about many aspects of your company because you interface with different departments.

There are many extras for salespeople. For example, in an effort to increase sales, many companies hold sales contests, with prizes of furniture, cruises, vacations, and appliances given to top salespeople. So some salespeople have good salaries and excellent fringes.

Educational Paths

Many employers desire employees with college degrees, but many salespeople have obtained employment with high school diplomas. Those with some previous sales experience may have the necessary experience to land sales positions. You can start at a small manufacturer by convincing your prospective employer of your sales ability and desire to enter the field. After you're hired and have gained significant experience, you can move on to middle-sized or large companies.

Job Outlook

The *Occupational Outlook Handbook* reports that "industrial firms, chain stores, and institutions that purchase large quantities of goods at one time frequently buy directly from manufacturers. The need for sales workers should continue as manufacturers emphasize sales activities to compete for the growing number of accounts."

Professional Association

For more information, write to:

Sales and Marketing Executives of Greater New York
114 E. 32nd Street
Suite 1301
New York, NY 10016

Salary Information

According to the *Occupational Outlook Handbook*, the most recent median annual earnings for manufacturer's sales workers were $23,400. Top sales workers earned more than $44,000; the middle 50 percent earned between $16,600 and $33,800 a year.

Skills Needed by a Manufacturer's Salesperson

Ability to:

1. Sell

2. Develop a sales system

3. Communicate both orally and in writing

4. Make contacts

5. Work independently

6. Be aggressive

7. Manage time

8. Analyze customers' needs

9. Make recommendations

10. Advise

11. Appraise situations

12. Calculate

13. Collect payments

14. Talk on the telephone

15. Deal with pressure

16. Meet with the public

17. Evaluate

18. Know the art of displaying products

19. Estimate costs

20. Handle complaints

21. Initiate

22. Observe

23. Obtain information

24. Persuade

15

Beauty Careers

Cosmetologists: Beauty Preservers

The fast-paced cosmetology field can offer you many career opportunities if you're a creative individual who has the forethought to expand her opportunities. It is no longer a field to view narrowly. Traditionally, most cosmetologists worked in salons, and their career opportunities ended there. Today, however, their career horizons have expanded to include other areas of the field. Some cosmetologists work in the retailing field as salespersons, assistant buyers, or buyers in the cosmetic departments of retail firms. Others work in direct sales as beauty consultants for multilevel marketing cosmetic companies.

There are others who work for cosmetic manufacturing firms as representatives, educational specialists and trainers, marketing representatives, trade technicians, or research assistants. Still others are hair stylists and makeup artists in the television, motion picture, and theater industries or work for commercial photographers. And other cosmetologists work in the beauty journalism field as editorial assistants, editors, free-lance writers, or consultants.

U.S. Department of Labor, Bureau of Labor Statistics, *Occupational Outlook Handbook*, 1986.

More than half a million people work as cosmetologists. Many began their careers as assistant hair stylists and then moved into careers as stylists, wig stylists, hair-straightening specialists, scalp and hair specialists, hair-coloring technicians, facial experts (aestheticians), makeup artists, or manicurists. Experienced cosmetologists often move into salon management or supervision or become salon owners. Others branch out into other areas in the cosmetics field.

As more and more of this society's people want to look better, cosmetology will continue to be a field where you can carve an interesting career path. Best opportunities are for the trendy pacesetter who lives in a major city like New York or Los Angeles.

Educational Paths

You must be licensed to be a cosmetologist. State licensing requirements vary, but generally you must be at least 16 years of age, be a graduate of a state-licensed cosmetology school, and pass a physical examination. In some states, you can take a one- or two-year apprenticeship in lieu of a cosmetology school program.

You can train to become a cosmetologist at either a public or private vocational school. This daytime training usually takes from six months to a year for full-time students; evening courses usually require more time.

After graduation from an accredited program, you must take a state licensing examination consisting of written and practical parts. In some states, you may also have to take an oral examination. And in some states, you must take a separate examination to get a manicurist or skin-care license.

Job Outlook

Job openings for cosmetologists are "expected to be plentiful throughout the mid-1990s," says the U.S. Department of Labor, Bureau of Labor Statistics.

Professional Association

For more information, write to:

National Hairdressers and
  Cosmetologists Association
3510 Olive Street
St. Louis, MO 63103

Salary Information

In 1986 experienced cosmetologists made between $18,000 and $24,000 a year; beginners made between $12,000 and $24,000; some earned over $30,000 according to the *Occupational Outlook Handbook*. Salaries for cosmetologists are based on commissions or wages and tips, and earnings are based on the size and location of the salon.

Skills Needed by a Cosmetologist

Ability to:

1. Be congenial

2. Meet the public

3. Be creative

4. Be thorough

5. Explain procedures or different selection of styles to customers

6. Analyze hair, skin, or nails

7. Cut, shampoo, straighten, or style hair

8. Make appointments

9. Manage salon
10. Continually educate oneself about trends in the field
11. Create new styles
12. Deal with pressure
13. Make decisions
14. Set prices
15. Be a good listener
16. Observe
17. Motivate clients to take better care of themselves
18. Persuade
19. Use cosmetology instruments
20. Order supplies
21. Follow through and get the job done

16

Leisure Careers

Hotel and Motel Assistants: The Innkeeper

The smooth running of any large hotel or motel is due in part to the hotel or motel manager's efficiency. She is responsible for the supervision of day-to-day operations and supervises the accounting, marketing, personnel, security, housekeeping, and maintenance departments. The buck stops with her because she is ultimately responsible for customer satisfaction.

The hotel and motel industry is a good field to enter and opportunities in it are expected to continue growing because more and more people are traveling on business, vacation, or personal trips. It is, therefore, a thriving business with many career opportunities.

One of the top honchos in this business is the general manager. But besides being a general manager, you can be a resident manager, assistant manager, executive housekeeper, front-office manager, catering manager, hostess, and so on. If you have the right

U.S. Department of Labor, Bureau of Labor Statistics, *Occupational Outlook Handbook*, 1986.

skills, experience, and training, you can work in sales, purchasing, personnel, tour or convention planning, or public relations.

And there are other jobs: room clerk, reservation clerk, media specialist, designer, telephone operator, executive cook, pantry supervisor, and accounting worker.

One entry-level position, like reservation clerk, is a good stepping-stone to more advanced positions. Another good training job is front-desk clerk.

Educational Paths

If you want to move into hotel management and assistant management positions, your experience in the field is given greatest weight. Some large hotels have training programs that will enable you to learn the business by working in various jobs. However, some employers prefer people with college degrees. Others will pay for their employees to get formal training in the field.

If you want to take formal training, you can take a two-year program leading to an associate degree in hotel and restaurant management at a junior or community college or technical institution.

You may also want to continue your training at a four-year bachelor's program for optimum career leverage. Over 100 colleges and universities offer degrees in the field.

Job Outlook

The *Occupational Outlook Handbook* says, "Employment of salaried hotel managers is expected to grow faster than the average for all occupations through the mid-1990s." This outlook is based on the predicted growth of hotels and motels.

Professional Association

For more information, write to:

American Hotel and Motel Association
888 Seventh Avenue
New York, NY 10019

Salary Information

According to the Department of Labor, Bureau of Labor Statistics, in 1985 general managers made total compensation packages that ranged from $35,000 for those who worked in small hotels to over $95,000 for those who worked in large hotels. Resident managers made between $25,000 for those who worked in small hotels to $55,000 for those who worked in large hotels.

Skills Needed by a Hotel Manager or Assistant

Ability to:

1. Meet and deal with the public

2. Be self-disciplined

3. Organize

4. Concentrate

5. Do detailed work

6. Supervise

7. Deal with stress

8. Follow through

9. Coordinate

10. Handle complaints
11. Troubleshoot
12. Cope with emergencies
13. Communicate orally and in writing
14. Make decisions
15. Administer
16. Analyze and size up situations
17. Anticipate problems
18. Solve problems
19. Make arrangements
20. Work on a team
21. Deal with pressure
22. Delegate
23. Endure
24. Evaluate
25. Calculate
26. Budget

17

An Entrepreneurial Career

Starting a Business: Owning a Piece of the Rock

Grab the entrepreneurial spirit and release yourself from the drudgery of a nine-to-five job. With a little ingenuity, an often-small investment, a lot of savvy, and hard work, you can join the ranks of today's successful business owners.

The road to entrepreneurial success won't be easy, but you can succeed like the thousands of others who have started businesses. It's much easier today to be a business success, because there is an abundance of help available like the Small Business Administration (SBA), Minority Business Development Agency (MBDA), and other agencies that help women and others get started.

With a marketable idea, a bit of luck, and some muscle work, you can own one of the more interesting businesses, like those devoted to catering, word processing and typing, gofering, publishing, advertising, public relations, art dealing, nursing registry, retailing cookies, balloon sales, photography, real estate, travel, computers, import and export, cosmetics, car rental, information processing, copying, and a host of other endeavors.

Let's look at how to create your business step-by-step.

Creating a Surefire Business Idea and Targeting Potential Customers

Deciding on a marketable business idea is the first step toward entrepreneurship. Every day, someone comes up with good business ideas.

Think of something that interests you or something that you can do well. For example, are you good at public relations? If so, start a public relations firm. Can you write good résumés? Why not open a résumé-writing service? If you're good at planning and coordinating conferences, start a conference-planning consulting firm. If you're a top-notch fund-raiser, then open a fund-raising consulting firm. Do you know how to successfully change careers? Then show others how to change theirs in your own career consulting firm. Opening a marketable business that incorporates something you like or can do well is ideal.

You think your idea is good and marketable, but does the public? It's time to find out by doing some market research. If you have the money, you may want to hire a market-research firm. However, most budding entrepreneurs can't afford the services of these firms and must do their own research. This can be accomplished by designing and mailing out questionnaires or by testing your product by placing ads in newspapers or magazines. For example, you may have a small publishing company that has a booklet showing people how to invest in real estate. To test your market, you may put a small ad in your local paper and gauge the response. Or you may go door-to-door sampling opinions or canvassing in local shopping malls to determine customer preferences. Many new business owners have been successful with this method.

Regardless of the method that you use, make sure you do some market research. It will save you both time and money.

Determining Your Business Form

Now determine your company's business form. Will it be an individual proprietorship, a partnership, or a corporation?

As an individual proprietor, you will have complete control over financing and business decisions. There are, however, disadvantages to this type of ownership including the financial responsibilities and debts until the business is solvent, and being responsible for paying income tax and social security deductions.

If you decide to get a partner or partners, both or all of you will share in business decisions. But you will also be collectively responsible for paying income taxes and social security deductions. A major advantage of partnerships is that the partners can share each other's level of expertise for the good of the business. A major disadvantage is that both, or all, of the partners must be harmonious or from the same "school of thought," or problems and ultimately business failure can occur.

To run a corporation, you must petition the state. The advantages of a corporation are that it is responsible for all debts instead of the individual owners or partners, and all federal, state, and local taxes are paid by the corporation.

A good accountant or tax attorney will be able to help you further explore the advantages and disadvantages of each business form. Carefully choose the best business form for you, and help ensure your business's success.

Getting Your Start-up Capital

Getting start-up capital may be the most difficult step in starting a business. Most people are somewhat naive about raising business capital, and so they turn to banks. Yet most banks are very conservative and generally give business loans to established businesses with proven track records.

Another problem is that some new entrepreneurs approach banks without having sound business plans. Without a plan, you probably won't be able to get financing. A business plan is a very well thought-out proposal. It includes an analysis of your company, taking into account the risks involved, your competition, marketing strategies and procedures, your staff's expertise, a cash flow analysis, and so on.

Even with a good business plan, you may still be turned down for bank financing. In this case, try soliciting friends, relatives, private investors, venture capitalists, or a government agency like the SBA (which guarantees business loans through banks). If you qualify, the SBA may guarantee 90 percent of a bank's loan to your business. In some very few instances, the SBA will make direct loans to business owners. The SBA also gives business ownership seminars and offers counseling through SCORE.

Managing Your Business

After your business has opened, make sure you have the management expertise to keep it strong and alive. Many businesses fail because of their owners' inability to run a business. To help, become familiar with basic accounting procedures, purchase orders, inventories, record keeping, stock turnovers, overstocks, markdowns, balance sheets, and profit and loss statements; or get an accountant to assist. And take business courses at your local junior or community college or university in accounting procedures, business management procedures, and so forth.

Professional Associations or Agencies

For more information, write to:

Small Business Administration
1441 L Street, NW
Washington, D.C. 20416
(or contact your local office)

American Women's Economic Development Corporation
60 East 42nd Street
New York, NY 10065

National Association of Women Business Owners
1722 Connecticut Avenue
Washington, D.C. 20009

In addition, minority women can write to:

National Association of Black Women Entrepreneurs
P.O. Box 1375
Detroit, MI 48231

American Association of Black Women Entrepreneurs
2300 South Elm/Eugene Street
Greensboro, NC 27406

Skills Needed by an Entrepreneur

Ability to:

1. Communicate both verbally and in writing
2. Manage company
3. Know business, product, and market
4. Sell
5. Supervise others
6. Delegate responsibility
7. Organize
8. Manage time
9. Do basic accounting procedures
10. Prioritize
11. Be a good administrator
12. Analyze
13. Appraise situations
14. Make sound decisions
15. Solve problems

16. Troubleshoot
17. Keep records
18. Persuade
19. Handle complaints
20. Do detail work
21. Be imaginative
22. Have vision
23. Write proposals
24. Interview
25. Deal with pressure
26. Work long hours
27. Negotiate

PART THREE

Getting That Sheepskin

18

Going or Returning to College

It is true that the more education you have, the more likely you are to be employed and work in a better-paying job. But many people didn't have a chance to go to college. Some were pushed into the work force because their families needed their financial help. Others married and raised families. Other women, like those belonging to minority groups, were told in high school that they weren't "college material," and that they should pursue secretarial work. Still others went to college but didn't complete their studies.

Today you may feel overwhelmed by going or returning to college. Where will the money come from? How will you fit studies into an already busy life? You are lucky because there are so many educational programs at both traditional colleges and universities and in nontraditional academic programs geared to help students in the work force. There are "schools without walls," "weekend colleges," "continuing education," and a host of other programs available to you.

First, let's talk about the more traditional college programs, associate and bachelor's degree programs.

Junior and Community Colleges

There are many junior and community colleges throughout the country. Their programs include studies in nursing, data processing, accounting, word processing, liberal arts, restaurant and hotel management, engineering technology, and so on. Some have certificate programs in areas like word processing.

Once you complete the regular curriculum at a junior or community college, you generally receive the degree of an associate in arts (A.A.) or an associate in applied science (A.A.S.). You normally must take from 65 to 68 credits, and this can generally be completed in two years (full-time). Part-timers take longer to complete their studies.

Let's look at a typical associate degree program. This one is at Bronx Community College in the Bronx, New York:

Academic area: Nursing

Length of time to complete program: Two years (full-time)

Degree to be earned: Associate in applied science (A.A.S.)

Number of credits needed to complete program: 65–68

Degree leads to: A.A.S. degree and eligibility to take the RN licensure examination given by the State of New York. Those with 2.5 averages are eligible to enter four-year City University of New York institutions.

Example of courses:

Dept. & no.	Course title	Credit
	PRE-NURSING SEMESTER	
Eng 13	Fundamental composition	3
Psy 11	Psychology	3
CMS 11	Fundamental communications	3
Bio 23	Human anatomy & physiology	4
	Total	13

Example of courses (Continued)

Dept. & no.	Course title	Credit
	FIRST SEMESTER	
Nur 31	Essential process of nursing	4
Bio 24	Human anatomy & physiology	4
PEA	Physical ed. (choose one)	1
CHM 14 or MTH 12	Intro. to chemistry, or intro. to mathematical thought	3–4
	Total	12–13
	SECOND SEMESTER	
Nur 32	Major health problems & clinical nursing activities 1 (Relatedness)	3
Nur 33	Foundations of nursing skills/critical situations	4
Bio 28	Bacteriology	3
Soc 11	Sociology	3
	Total	13

(continued)

Example of courses (Continued)

Dept. & no.	Course title	Credit
	THIRD SEMESTER	
Nur 34	Major health problems & clinical nursing activities 11 (Long-term problems: motor & neurological)	4
Nur 35	Major health problems & clinical nursing activities 111 (reproduction & the young family)	4
MUS 10 or Art 10	Music survey, or art survey	1
	Elective	3–4
	Total	12–13
	FOURTH SEMESTER	
Nur 36	Major health problems—medical & surgical problems of adults and children	4
Nur 37	Clinical nursing activities—medical & surgical problems of adults and children	4
Nur 38	Management in nursing health promotion	4
	Elective	3–4
	Total	15–16

Or you may be interested in pursuing a certificate program at a junior or community college. For example, if you are interested in word processing, you may be able to get into a one-year certificate program. Below is a sample certificate program at La Guardia Community College:

Academic area : Secretarial science

Length of time to complete program: One year

Degree earned: Certificate in word processing

Number of credits needed to complete program: 33

Example of courses:

Dept. & no.	Course title	Credit
	FIRST QUARTER	
Engl 101	Composition 1	3
HUC 101	Oral communication	3
SEC 140	Typewriting 1	2
	Total	8
	SECOND QUARTER	
AMM 101	Introduction to business	3
SEC 141	Typewriting 11	2
SEC 144	Concepts of word processing	2
	Total	7
	THIRD QUARTER	
Engl 112	Writing for business	3
SEC 142	Typewriting 111	2
SEC 145	Word processing 1	2
SEC 147	Administration of word processing center	3
	Total	10

(*continued*)

Example of courses (Continued)

Dept. & no.	Course title	Credit
	FOURTH QUARTER	
	Elective (liberal arts)	3
SEC 146	Word processing	2
SEC 148	Simulation of word processing	3
	Total	8
	Program Total	33

There are many advantages to attending a junior or community college, but there are also some disadvantages. Carefully weigh the advantages and disadvantages of attending a junior or community college rather than a four-year college or university or nontraditional program:

Advantages

1. Some junior and community college programs (often known as "career programs") lead to immediate employment. For example, a nursing program at a junior or community college can lead to your fulfillment of the requirements to take state nursing examinations for registered nurses (check with your state for eligibility requirements). Or you may take a data processing program, and after completion you may be eligible for an entry-level position.

2. It takes less time to complete the academic requirements needed for an A.A. or A.A.S. than for a B.A. or B.S. After two or more years (full-time), you are eligible for a degree. This is particularly appealing for those in "career programs."

3. Many returning-to-school adults choose community colleges. Since many older students attend community colleges, you will be among your peers.

Disadvantages

1. After completing your studies at a two-year junior or community college, you may not be able to transfer and complete your studies at a college or university.

Colleges and Universities (programs leading to a bachelor's degree)

Programs in colleges and universities usually take four years (full-time) to complete, and lead to a bachelor of arts or bachelor of science degree. But, there are other types of degree programs. Traditionally, graduation from one of these colleges or universities has meant movement into better-paying jobs. It has also meant the possibility of doing graduate work or study at a professional school (such as law school or medical school).

At a college or university, you can take a wide variety of majors, including psychology, computer science, communications, engineering, economics, business administration, theater, education, nursing, liberal arts, and many more. Below is a typical program for a college or university program at Marymount Manhattan College:

Academic area: Business management

Length of time to complete program: Four years (full-time)

Degree earned: B.A.

Number of credits needed to complete program: 120

Example of courses:

Dept. & no.	Course title	Credit
	COLLEGE REQUIREMENTS	
College skills 012	Composition or exemption	0
Math 007	Developmental mathematics or exemption	0
Humanities 101 & 102	Critical thinking I & II	6
Liberal arts program	Philosophy, psychology, or religious studies	3
	General science, biology, chemistry, or physics	3
	History, sociology, or political science	3
	Communications, English, a foreign language, or international literature	3
	Art, music, dance, theater, or film	6
	Liberal Studies Seminar	3
	DIVISIONAL REQUIREMENTS	
Math 111 or 113	Precalculus or quantitative reasoning	3–4
Math 112 or 150	Calculus or applied quantitative techniques	3
Data processing 117	Introduction to data processing	3

Example of courses (Continued)

Dept. & no.	Course title	Credit
	MAJOR REQUIREMENTS	
Business 200	Principles of management	3
Business 210	Marketing	3
Accounting 215 & 217	Principles of accounting I & II	8
Business 224	Statistics I	3
Business 275	Business law I & II	6
Business 309	Financial management	3
Business 330	Computer applications in business management and accounting	3
Business 347	Corporate finance	3
Economics 205	Principles of economics I	3
Economics 207	Principles of economics II	3
	Special interest sequences including one 400-level course	12
	OTHER REQUIREMENTS	
	Open electives	30–31
	Program Total	120

There are many advantages and disadvantages to attending a college or university:

Advantages

1. Many colleges and universities have special programs to accommodate the special needs of older students, such as "weekend colleges," offerings of "credit for life experience," and so on.

2. Your company may reimburse you for attending a college or university or for further education.

3. People who graduate from colleges or universities have a lower unemployment rate and make more during their work lives.

4. Many colleges and universities offer special combination programs in which undergraduate and graduate courses are combined, resulting in, for example, a B.A.–M.P.A. (bachelor and master of public administration) degree.

Disadvantages

1. It's a long haul to complete a degree program at a college or university. This is especially true for part-time students. But any goal that is worthwhile takes some struggle and sacrifice.

2. Some colleges and universities cost a great deal to attend. But there is financial aid available for eligible students. And many companies reimburse employees who are studying in job-related programs.

Correspondence Schools and Independent Study

You can get college credit through correspondence or independent study sponsored by member institutions of the Division of Independent Study of the National University Extension Association. If you acquire college credit through this method, you will be sent college course materials from the affiliated college or university. Once completed, you will return assignments to be graded.

Remember, the standards used in classrooms are used in grading the material. For more information, send for the *NUEA Guide to Independent Study through Correspondence Instruction* ($4.50 plus $1.25 postage and handling) from Peterson's Guides, Book Order Department, P.O. Box 2123, Princeton, NJ 08540. Or for information about NUEA's program, write to them at NUEA, Suite 360, One Dupont Circle, Washington, D.C. 20036.

You can also take courses from private correspondence schools. Some colleges will give you credit for them. But you should verify this with the college to which the credit will be transferred. You should also determine whether the school you're paying is accredited. For more information, check with the National Home Study Council for their directory as well as for other materials on home study courses. The National Home Study Council is located at 1601 18th Street, NW, Washington, D.C. 20009.

College Credit by Examination

You may have gained knowledge from many sources: reading, on-the-job training, hobbies, avocations, correspondence courses, and so on. Based on your knowledge of certain subjects, you may be able to pass examinations and ultimately get college credit.

There are several types of proficiency examinations: Regents College Examinations (RCEs), College-Level Examination Program (CLEP), Graduate Record Examination (GRE) Subject tests, DANTES, and University End-of-Course Examinations.

Regents College Examinations (RCEs)

These examinations are given in several areas: education, arts and sciences, secretarial science, nursing, and business. If you live in New York State, RCEs are given several times a year. If you live outside of New York State, these examinations are known as ACT

PEP tests, and they are administered by the American College Testing Program. ACT PEP tests are given at testing centers across the United States. If you are taking RCEs in any area except nursing (which has prerequisites), they are open to anyone who applies. Even if you fail an examination, you can retake it later on.

College-Level Examination Program (CLEP)

The College-Level Examination Program is administered through the College Entrance Examination Board. CLEP has two types of tests—general examinations and subject examinations. General examinations measure your knowledge in areas such as humanities, English composition, mathematics, natural science, and social science and history. Subject examinations test knowledge learned in thirty subjects.

Graduate Record Examination (GRE)

Graduate Record Examination Subject tests measure your comprehensive understanding and mastery of subject matter in major fields. For example, if you are working toward a bachelor's degree in liberal arts, you may take a GRE Subject test and receive a total of thirty credits in an area of concentration. These tests are given four times a year across the country.

Defense Activity for Non-Traditional Education Support (DANTES)

DANTES is responsible for the educational and testing functions of the U.S. Armed Forces Institute. It administers examinations called DANTES Subject Standardized Tests (DSSTs) and oversees other tests like the RCEs and ACT PEP and CLEP tests for military personnel. For more information, contact your education officer at the military installation where you're stationed.

University End-of-Course Examinations

There are two university-sponsored programs where students can get college credit through examination. One program is the Ohio University Course Credit by Examination (Tupper Hall, Ohio University, Athens, OH 45701); the other is the University of North Carolina Independent Study (Abernethy Hall, 002A, Chapel Hill, NC 27514). There are several other programs of this type, but these two are perhaps the most extensive.

Regents College Degrees

If you are a self-motivated student, this accredited, nontraditional degree program may be for you. The Regents College Degrees program is designed to meet the academic needs of students across the United States and in military bases around the world. It has helped more than 30,000 students receive degrees. You can earn an associate or bachelor's degree in business, liberal arts, technology, or many other subject areas. All degrees granted through this program are accredited by the Middle States Association of Colleges and Schools and by the New York State Board of Regents. In addition, all nursing degrees are accredited by the National League of Nursing.

The Regents College Degrees program is a unique alternative program that lets you earn credit for college through various methods, such as independent study, correspondence course study, proficiency examinations, and prior college credit. Its main goal is to assess and document learning instead of teaching students in a traditional college setting.

If you want to pursue a degree through this program, you can put together a program that includes several of the methods used in getting college credit. For example, if you have taken college courses at a traditional college or university or earned college credit by taking correspondence courses, you may use some of the credits earned toward a Regents College Degree. The college or university where courses are taken must be accredited by one of the six regional accrediting agencies like the Middle States Association of Colleges and Schools.

You can also include approved college-level proficiency examinations or courses that have been evaluated and recommended for college credit taken through military service school courses. Or you may use the special assessment method of getting college credit. In this method, you are usually required to take oral examinations that are administered in Albany, New York, and will measure your college-level knowledge from experience or independent study.

You can also get credit from business-, industry-, or government-sponsored courses. But you can only use courses that have been evaluated and recommended by the New York National Program on Noncollegiate Sponsored Instruction (PONSI) or the American Council on Education's PONSI. You can also get credit through approved nursing performance examinations.

If you want to earn an associate degree in liberal arts through the Regents College Degrees program, you must complete a total of sixty credits. Upon satisfactory completion, you will be awarded an associate in arts degree (A.A.) or an associate in science degree (A.S.). Afterward you will be eligible to pursue a bachelor's degree through the program.

If you are pursuing a bachelor's degree in liberal arts, you can pursue a bachelor of arts (B.A.) or bachelor of science (B.S.) degree. Each requires the successful completion of 120 credits.

Or you may pursue an associate or bachelor's degree in business. Upon completion of the required sixty credits, you will be awarded an associate in science degree in business. Upon completion of 120 credits, you will be awarded a bachelor of science degree in business.

For those interested in degrees in technology, you can get one of the following degrees:

> Associate in science in electronics technology
> Bachelor of science in electronics technology
> Bachelor of science in computer technology
> Associate in science in computer software
> Bachelor of science in computer software
> Associate in science in nuclear technology
> Bachelor of science in nuclear technology

Nursing students can receive three types of degrees: associate in science, associate in applied science, or bachelor of science degree. (All are accredited by the National League of Nursing and the Middle States Association of Colleges and Schools.) After graduation, you will be eligible for licensing in most states. But it is important to check with the state board of nursing in the state where you intend to practice for specific licensing requirements.

After completing the Regents College Degrees program bachelor's degree, you may be eligible for graduate school. Here is a partial list of some of the schools that have accepted Regents College graduates: Adelphi University, American University, Boston University, Columbia University, Cornell University, Harvard University, Meharry Medical College, New York University, Rutgers, State University of New Jersey, Syracuse University, Temple University, University of California, University of Chicago, University of Michigan, Washington University, and Yale University.

Thomas A. Edison College

Thomas A. Edison College offers a national program like the Regents College Degrees program. Thomas A. Edison gives college credit for various documented learning, like military education, proficiency examinations, individualized assessments of skills and knowledge that can't be properly evaluated by testing, noncollegiate courses that have been evaluated and given college credit equivalent, and courses taken at other colleges. For more information, write to Thomas A. Edison State College, CN 545, 101 West State Street, Trenton, NJ 08625.

Credit for Noncollege Learning

If you have taken a course through a labor union, government agency, community organization, the military, or a volunteer or professional organization, you may be able to get college credit for it. The Office of Educational Credit at the American Council on Education evaluates these courses and recommends the number of equivalent college credits. In their booklet, *The National Guide to Educational Credit for Training Programs,* you will find the course descriptions and equivalent semester hours they are equal to. This book costs $37.50 and can be ordered by calling Macmillan Publishing at (800) 257-5755.

Credit for Experience

If you are or have been a volunteer, you can now get college credit for volunteerism skills. The Task Force of Volunteer Accreditation of the Council of National Organizations for Adult Education has a series of "I Can" lists. Its book "I Can: A Tool for Assessing Skills Acquired through Volunteer Experience" has information regarding I Can lists for twelve volunteer titles. It can be purchased through Ramco Associates at 406 West 31st Street, New York, NY 10001.

The Educational Testing Service in conjunction with the Council of National Organizations for Adult Education developed a workbook with more I Can lists to help people identify volunteer and homemaker skills. The book *How to Get Credit for What You Have Learned as a Homemaker or Volunteer* is $5.00 and can be ordered from the Accrediting Women's Competencies T-154, Educational Testing Service, Princeton, NJ 08541.

Career Development Women's Studies

The State University of New York (SUNY) in Purchase offers a special program, Career Development Women's Studies, for those women with some or no college. This program has helped many women without college degrees move into managerial positions. Courses help women boost confidence, learn speaking skills, write better, and tackle math. For more information about the program, contact the Career Development Women's Studies Course, Cornell University, N.Y.S.S.I.L.R., SUNY at Purchase, Administration Building, Room 310, Purchase NY 10577.

Similar programs may also be available from the University of California Extension in Los Angeles; Washburn University in Topeka; Inver Hills Community College in St. Paul, Minnesota; Limestone College in Gaffney, South Carolina; Miami-Dade Community College; St. Louis Community College in Missouri; and Parkersburg Community College in West Virginia.

For more information about the programs mentioned in this chapter, write to:

ACT PEP Tests
American College Testing
  Program
P.O. Box 168
Iowa City, IA 52243

CLEP Tests
College Level Examination
  Program
Box 1822
Princeton, NJ 08541

DANTES
(contact the education officer
at your military installation)

GRE Subject Tests
Graduate Record Examinations
Educational Testing Service
CN 6000
Princeton, NJ 08541-6000

Regents College Degrees
Cultural Education Center
Albany, NY 12230

Regents College Examinations
Cultural Education Center
Albany, NY 12230

APPENDIX A
OTHER JOBS FOR WOMEN WITHOUT COLLEGE DEGREES

Job title	Educational paths	Job outlook
Retail trade sales worker	You'll probably learn retail trade sales work on-the-job; some larger establishments will train you in formal programs. Some retail experience is helpful in getting jobs in the field.	Opportunities in this area will grow about as fast as the average for all workers. But entry-level retail positions are excellent stepping-stone jobs to more lucrative retail positions with better employment opportunities.
Social service aide	Most of these workers are trained on-the-job and placed in positions according to their educational background. For example, a high school graduate may be assigned to clerical duties. On the other hand, those with college degrees may perform some of a social worker's duties.	Employment is "expected to grow faster than the average for all occupations as social welfare programs expand and as aides perform tasks formerly handled by professional personnel," says the U.S. Department of Labor, Bureau of Labor Statistics.
Funeral director and embalmer	This is a very lucrative field. High school graduates with mortuary science school training are welcome in this field. Requirements include being at least 21 years of age, having a high school diploma or GED, serving an internship, and passing a state board examination. About 50% of all states require that you have 1 year or more of college plus the mortuary science school	Employment opportunities in the field are expected to remain the same.

training. You can get 1-year mortuary science training in vocational schools or 2-year programs at junior or community colleges. The majority of states require funeral directors and embalmers to be licensed.

Employment in this field is expected to increase about as fast as the average for all occupations through the mid-1990s.

Teacher aide

Your state or city will determine the requirements for this position. Some aides are high school graduates; others don't have high school diplomas; still others have college training. You may get on-the-job training or formal training at a junior or community college. To get the competitive employment edge, get some work experience with children.

Medical record technician and clerk

If you have secretarial skills, you can become a medical record clerk and learn routine tasks through a 1-month on-the-job training program. You can also take a correspondence course in medical transcription that is offered by the American Medical Record Association (AMRA). This course will be very helpful in terms of getting employment.

Employment opportunities will be very good for medical record technicians and clerks, as "employment is expected to grow much faster than the average for all occupations," reports the U.S. Department of Labor, Bureau of Labor Statistics.

(continued)

Job title	Educational paths	Job outlook
Operating room technician	If you want to enter this field, get training at a vocational or technical school, hospital, or community or junior college. Usually this training will take from 9 months to 1 year, but you can get an associate degree at a junior college. Some technicians, however, receive on-the-job training that usually takes from 6 weeks to 1 year depending on the worker's qualifications. If you have work experience as a nursing aide or practical nurse, you'll have the competitive edge.	Employment opportunities are expected to grow about as fast as the average for all occupations for these technicians. Opportunities for those with 2-year community and junior college associate degrees are best.
Optometric assistant	Most of these workers are trained on-the-job, but you can get training in a 1- or 2-year course at a junior college. If you are a high school graduate and know office procedures, you will get preferential treatment for employment.	The U.S. Department of Labor, Bureau of Labor Statistics, says, "Employment is expected to grow faster than the average for all occupations due to greater demand for eye care services. Job opportunities for persons who have completed a formal training program should be excellent."
Radiologic (x-ray) technologist	To enter the field, you must complete a 2-year training program in x-ray technology	The U.S. Department of Labor, Bureau of Labor Statistics, says,

	at a hospital, medical school, college, junior college, or vocational school. You may also further your education by taking a bachelor's or master's degree program.	"Employment is expected to grow faster than the average for all occupations as x-ray equipment is increasingly used to diagnose and treat diseases." Competition for these jobs is great.
Engineering and science technician	You should have some specialized training (1–4 years full-time study) at a technical institute, junior college, or community college, extension division of a college or university, or vocational technical high school. You can also get on-the-job training, attend school on a part-time basis, or take correspondence school courses.	There will be plentiful opportunities for engineering and science technicians, and "employment is expected to increase faster than the average for all occupations," says the U.S. Department of Labor, Bureau of Labor Statistics.
Business machine repairer	Most workers begin as trainees and learn on-the-job. Many who work for manufacturers and franchise dealers generally receive training at manufacturers' schools. Or you can get training at independent repair shops. Some employers want high school graduates to have at least 1 year of technical training in basic electricity or electronics.	The U.S. Department of Labor, Bureau of Labor Statistics, says, "Employment is expected to grow faster than the average for all occupations as more machines are used to handle an increasing volume of paperwork."

(continued)

Job title	Educational paths	Job outlook
Respiratory therapy worker	There are three types of workers in this field: technicians, therapists, and assistants. If you want to become a technician or therapist, you must get formal training. To become a technician, you will need to take a 12-month program at a college, university, junior college, or hospital. Or you may take training that will last 18 to 24 months or take a 2-year program leading to an associate degree.	"Employment is expected to grow *much* faster than the average for all occupations due to new applications of respiratory therapy in treating diseases," says the U.S. Department of Labor, Bureau of Labor Statistics.
Dental laboratory technician	You will probably learn this work through on-the-job training that takes about 4 to 5 years. Or you can learn this occupation at a few vocational schools or at an accredited 2-year program (one accredited by the American Dental Association) at a junior college or technical school. After your training, you may need approximately 3 years of experience to become a fully qualified technician.	"Employment is expected to grow faster than the average for all occupations due to the expansion of dental prepayment plans and increasing numbers of older persons who require dentures," reports the U.S. Department of Labor, Bureau of Labor Statistics.
Flight attendant	Major airlines train their flight attendants. This training generally takes 5 weeks. You must be a high school graduate, but those	Competition for these jobs is fierce, but employment opportunities are expected to increase.

	with 2 or more years of college or experience dealing with the public are preferred.	
Broadcast technician	Federal law dictates that anyone who operates broadcast transmitters in radio and television stations must have a restricted radio-telephone operator permit (no examination required). However, those who work with microwave or internal radio communications equipment must have a general radio-telephone operator license. You can get this license by passing a series of written examinations. The best way to train for the field is to get training in technical schools, junior or community colleges, or 4-year colleges and universities.	Jobs in this area are tough to get because competition is great. The U.S. Department of Labor, Bureau of Labor Statistics, predicts average growth in employment opportunities. Best employment bets are in smaller cities.
Drafter	To train for this field, take courses at a technical institution, junior or community college, extension division of a university, or vocational and technical high schools. You may also get on-the-job training in conjunction with part-time schooling or by taking a 3- or 4-year apprenticeship program.	The U.S. Department of Labor, Bureau of Labor Statistics, says, "Employment is expected to grow about as fast as the average for all occupations." This increase is due to the complexity of the designs for products and processes.

(continued)

Job title	Educational paths	Job outlook
Bookkeeping worker	Courses in mathematics, bookkeeping, and accounting will prepare you for the job. Business school or junior or community college course work will give you the competitive edge. Work experience in the field also makes you more marketable.	Employment prospects are expected to grow more slowly than average for all occupations throughout the 1990s. Job prospects should be good, nonetheless, in view of the large number of openings that will occur because of the need to replace workers who transfer to other occupations or stop working.
Secretary and stenographer	A high school diploma with some training at a business school or junior or community college is the best preparation. You must also be able to type 50 WPM or have a stenographic speed of 110 WPM.	Employment opportunities are expected to grow more slowly due to office automation.
Bartender	Formerly, an unlikely field for women, but this is rapidly changing. As a bartender, you will learn your trade through on-the-job training. Some states require bartenders to have health certificates saying they are free from contagious diseases. You may have to be bonded and at least 21 or 25 years of age.	As new restaurants, bars, hotels, and motels open, there will be an increased need for bartenders. Employment opportunities will be plentiful.

Cook and chef	If you have a flair for cooking or have worked as a kitchen helper or have had high school or vocational training in food preparation, you can get employment in the field. If you have training in the field, you'll have a competitive edge. Some states require cooks and chefs to have health certificates to certify that they are free from contagious diseases.	Employment in this field will be plentiful.
Plumber and pipe fitter	A 5-year apprenticeship is the recommended training, but many plumbers and pipe fitters learn as helpers on-the-job. A high school or vocational school background with courses in mathematics, drafting, physics, and chemistry can be helpful. In some cities, plumbers and pipe fitters must be licensed. Licensing requirements include taking a written examination.	"Employment is expected to grow as fast as the average for all occupations," says the U.S. Department of Labor, Bureau of Labor Statistics.
Carpenter	The best training bet is a 4-year apprenticeship. But most carpenters learn on-the-job, which is a longer process than through an apprenticeship. You can also learn some of the trade by taking some	The U.S. Department of Labor, Bureau of Labor Statistics, predicts, "Employment is expected to grow about as fast as the average for all occupations."

(continued)

297

Job title	Educational paths	Job outlook
	vocational school courses like carpentry, shop, mathematics, and mechanical drawing.	
Electrician (construction)	The most effective and recommended way to learn this trade is through a 4-year apprenticeship. But some electricians learn on-the-job as helpers. You may also take relevant courses at a vocational school such as electricity, mechanical drawing, science, and shop. The majority of cities require that you become licensed as an electrician. Licensing requirements include taking a written examination and demonstrating your skill.	Opportunities for electricians will "increase about as fast as the average," says the U.S. Department of Labor, Bureau of Labor Statistics.
Electronic home entertainment equipment repairer	If you've had training in electronics at a high school, vocational school, or technical school, you have a competitive edge in terms of getting employed.	"Employment is expected to increase about as fast as the average for all occupations as the number of home entertainment products increases," says the U.S. Department of Labor, Bureau of Labor Statistics.

Lithographer	An apprenticeship program is one way to enter the field. To be eligible for an apprenticeship, you should be a high school graduate. Many technical institutions, junior or community colleges, and colleges have 2-year programs in printing technology. Although apprenticeships and training are available in the field, most lithographers learn on-the-job.	Employment opportunities, particularly for those with post–high school training, are expected to grow about as fast as the average for all occupations through the mid-1990s.
Photographic laboratory worker	Most learn on-the-job, and most employers prefer high school graduates. On-the-job training for a particular laboratory procedure usually takes a few years.	The U.S. Department of Labor, Bureau of Labor Statistics, predicts, "Employment is expected to grow faster than the average for all occupations due to the increasing use of photography in business and government and the growing popularity of amateur photography."

Source: U.S. Department of Labor, Bureau of Labor Statistics, *Occupational Outlook Handbook*, 1986.

APPENDIX B
MORE JOBS FOR WOMEN
WITHOUT DEGREES

Actress
Air-conditioning, refrigeration, and heating mechanic
Air traffic controller
Airplane mechanic
Appliance repairer
Assembler
Automobile-body repairer
Automobile mechanic
Automobile painter
Automobile-parts-counter worker
Automobile salesperson
Automobile service assistant
Bank clerk
Bank teller
Barber
Blacksmith
Blue collar–worker supervisor
Boat-engine mechanic
Boiler tender
Boilermaking occupations
Bookbinder and bindery worker

Brick layer, stone mason, and marble setter
Building custodian
Cashier
Cement mason and terrazzo worker
Claim representative
Collection worker
Compositor
Conductor
Construction inspector
Construction laborer
Coremaker (metalworking)
Correction officer
Dancer
Diesel mechanic
Dining room attendant
Display worker (retail)
Drywall installer and finisher
EEG technician
EKG technician
Electric-sign repairer
Electroplater
Electrotyper
Farm-equipment mechanic
File clerk
Firefighter
Floral designer
Food-counter worker
Forestry technician
Forge-shop occupations
Furniture upholsterer
General machinist
Glazier (construction)
Guard
Homemaker (home health aide)
Hotel front-office clerk
Hotel housekeeper and assistant
Industrial-machinery repairer
Inspector (manufacturing)
Instrument maker (mechanical)

Instrument repairer
Insulation worker
Intercity bus driver
Interior decorator
Iron worker (structural, ornamental, and reinforcing iron worker;
   rigger; and machine mover)
Jeweler
Lather
Library technician and assistant
Local transit bus driver
Local truck driver
Locksmith
Locomotive engineer
Long-distance truck driver
Machine-tool operator
Mail carrier
Maintenance electrician
Meat cutter
Medical laboratory worker
Millwright
Molder
Motion-picture projectionist
Motorcycle mechanic
Musician
Nursing aide, orderly, and attendant
Office machine operator
Operating engineer (construction machinery operator)
Painter and paper hanger
Park, recreation, and leisure-service worker
Parking attendant
Patternmaker
Pest controller
Photoengraver
Piano and organ tuner and repairer
Plasterer
Plumber and pipe fitter
Police officer
Postal clerk
Power-truck operator

Printing press operator and assistant
Production painter
Receptionist
Reservation, ticket, and passenger agent
Roofer
Route driver
Setup worker (machine tools)
Sheet-metal worker
Shipping and receiving clerk
Shoe repairer
Signal department worker
Singer
State police officer
Station agent (railroad)
Stationary engineer
Statistical worker
Stock clerk
Surveyor
Taxicab driver
Telegrapher, telephoner, and tower operator
Telephone and PBX installer and repairer
Telephone equipment installer (central office)
Telephone line installer and cable slicer
Telephone operator
Tool-and-die maker
Truck mechanic and bus mechanic
Typist
Vending-machine mechanic
Waitress
Wastewater treatment plant operator (sewage plant operator)
Watch repairer
Welder

APPENDIX C
WOMEN'S BUSINESS
ORGANIZATIONS

American Business Women's
  Association
9100 Ward Parkway
P.O. Box 8728
Kansas City, MO 64114

American Nurses' Association
2420 Pershing Road
Kansas City, MO 64108

Black Career Women, Inc.
2015 Madison Road
Cincinnati, OH 45208

Coalition of Labor Union Women
National Office
15 Union Square
New York, NY 10003

Department for Professional
  Employees, AFLCIO
Committee on Salaried and
  Professional Women
815 16th Street, NW, #608
Washington, D.C. 20006

Communication Workers of
  America, Women's Activities
1925 K Street, NW
Washington, D.C. 20006

National Association of Bank
  Women
500 North Michigan Avenue
Chicago, IL 60611

National Association of Insurance
  Women
P.O. Box 4410
Tulsa, OK 74159

National Association of Negro
  Business and Professional
  Women's Clubs, Inc.
1806 New Hampshire Avenue,
  NW
Washington, D.C. 20009

Nine to Five
National Association of Working
  Women
1614 Superior, NW
Cleveland, OH 44113

National Council of Negro
  Women, Inc.
701 North Fairfax Street, No. 330
Alexandria, VA 22314

The National Federation of
  Business and
  Professional Women
2012 Massachusetts Avenue, NW
Washington, D.C. 20036

Women in Communications, Inc.
P.O. Box 9561
Austin, TX 78766

National Association for Female
  Executives, Inc.
1041 Third Avenue
New York, NY 10021

National Association of Colored
  Women's Clubs
5808 16th Street, NW
Washington, D.C. 20011

National Coalition of 100 Black
  Women
50 Rockefeller Plaza
Suite 46, Concourse Level
New York, NY 10020

SUGGESTED READING

Abarbanel, Karen, and Gonnie McClung Siegel: *Women's Workbook*, Warner Books, $2.50.

Anthony, Robert: *Put Your Money Where Your Mouth Is*, Berkeley Books, $3.50.

Appelbaum, Judith, and Nancy Evans: *How to Get Happily Published: A Complete and Candid Guide*, New American Library, $6.95.

Bayless, Hugh: *The Best Towns in America: A Where-to-Go-Guide for a Better Life*, Houghton Mifflin, $9.95.

Bear, John: *How to Get the Degree You Want: Bear's Guide to Non-Traditional College Degrees*, Ten Speed Press, $9.95.

Behr, Marion, and Wendy Lazar: *Women Working Home: The Homebased Business Guide and Directory*, Working Women Home, $12.95.

Biegelelsen, J. I.: *Job Resumes: How to Write Them, Present Them, Preparing for Interviews*, Grosset & Dunlap, $6.95.

Bird, Caroline: *The Two-Paycheck Marriage*, Pocket Books, $2.75.

Blanchard, Kenneth, and Spencer Johnson: *The One Minute Manager*, Morrow, $7.95.

Blaze, Wayne, Bill Hertzberg, Roy Krantz, and Al Lehrke: *Guide to Alternative Colleges and Universities*.

Blye, Robert W., and Gary Blake: *Dream Jobs*, Wiley, $8.95.

Bolles, Richard N.: *The Three Boxes of Life*, Ten Speed Press, $14.95.

————: *What Color Is Your Parachute?* Ten Speed Press, $8.95.

Brabec, Barbara: *Homemade Money: The Definitive Guide to Success in a Home Business*, Betterway Publications, $12.95.

Carroll, Mary Bridget: *Overworked and Underpaid*, Fawcett Books, $8.95.

Catalyst: *Marketing Yourself: The Catalyst Guide to Successful Resumes and Interviews*, Bantam Books, $3.50.

————: *Upward Mobility*, Warner Books, $3.95.

————: *What to Do with the Rest of Your Life: The Catalyst Career Guide for Women in the 80's*, Simon & Schuster, $16.95.

The College Board: *Paying for Your Education*, The College Board, New York, $7.95. (The College Board, 888 Seventh Avenue, New York, NY 10106).

Davidson, Peter: *Moonlighting*, McGraw-Hill, New York, $7.95.

Davis, George, and Glegg Watson: *Black Life in Corporate America: Swimming in the Mainstream*, Anchor Press/Doubleday, $14.95.

Denny, Jon S.: *Careers in Cable TV*, Barnes & Noble Books, $7.95.

Dible, Donald M.: *Up Your Own Organization*, Reston Publishing, $6.95.

Douglas, Martha C.: *Go for It! How to Get Your First Good Job*, Ten Speed Press, $5.95.

Ekstrom, Ruth B., Abigail M. Harris, and Marilaine E. Lookheed: *How to Get College Credit for What You Have Learned as a Homemaker and Volunteer*, Project Have Skills, Education Testing Service, $5.00.

Figler, Howard E.: *The Complete Job Search Handbook: Presenting the Skills You Need to Get Any Job, and Have a Good Time Doing It*, Holt, Rinehart & Winston, $5.95.

Gates, Anita: *90 Most Promising Careers for the 80's*, Monarch Press, $7.95.

Germann, Richard, and Peter Arnold: *Bernard Haldane Associates' Job and Career Building*, Ten Speed Press, $6.95.

Goldberg, Joan Rachel: *High Tech Career Strategies for Women*, Collier Books, $9.95.

Gross, Ronald: *The Independent Scholar's Handbook: How to Turn Your Interest in Any Subject into Expertise*, Addison-Wesley, $8.95.

Hagberg, Janet, and Richard Leider: *The Inventurers: Excursions in Life and Career Renewal*, Addison-Wesley, $9.95.

Haldane, Bernard, and Jean M. Haldane: *Job Finding Power*, Bernard Haldane, $8.75.

Half, Robert: *Robert Half on Hiring*, Crown, $15.95.

Haponski, William C., and Charles E. McCabe: *New Horizons: The Education and Career Planning Guide for Adults*, Peterson's Guides, $9.20.

Harragan, Betty Lehan: *Games Mother Never Taught You: Corporate Gamesmanship for Women*, Warner Books, $2.50.

Harrop, David: *Paychecks: Who Makes What? The Book That Tells You What Everybody Earns*, Harper & Row, $5.95.

Herbert, Tom, and John Coyne: *Getting Skilled*, Dutton, $4.95.

Holland, John L.: *Making Vocational Choices: A Theory of Careers*, Prentice-Hall, $15.95.

Irish, Richard K.: *Go Hire Yourself an Employer*, Anchor Press/Doubleday, $6.95.

Jackson, Tom: *Guerilla Tactics in the Job Market*, Bantam Books, $3.95.

————: *The Perfect Resume*, Anchor Press/Doubleday, $6.95.

Jessup, Claudia, and Genie Chipps: *The Woman's Guide to Starting a Business*, Holt, Rinehart & Winston, $4.95.

Johnson, Willis L. (ed.): *Directory of Special Programs for Minority Group Members: Career Information Services, Employment Skills Banks, Financial Aid Services*, Garrett Press, Garrett Park, MD, $19.00.

Kandel, Thelma: *What Women Earn*, Simon & Schuster, $6.95.

Kennedy, Marily Moats: *Career Knockouts, How to Battle Back*, Warner Books, $2.95.

————: *Office Politics: Seizing Power, Wielding Clout*, New Century, $10.95.

Kisiel, Marie: *Career Strategies for Secretaries*, Contemporary Books, $7.95.

Lathrop, Richard: *Who's Hiring Who*, Ten Speed Press, $5.95.

Leape, Martha P.: *The Harvard Guide to Careers*, Harvard University Press, $6.95.

Lee, Patricia: *The Complete Guide to Job Sharing*, Walker and Co., $6.95.

Lerner, Elaine, and C. B. Abbott: *The Way to Go—A Woman's Guide to Careers in Travel*, Warner Books, $6.95.

Maccoby, Michael: *The Games Man*, Bantam Books, $2.75.

Marks, Edith, and Adele Lewis: *Job Hunting for the Disabled*, Barron's Educational Services, $8.95.

Medley, H. Anthony: *Sweaty Palms: The Neglected Art of Being Interviewed*, Ten Speed Press, $7.95.

Mitchell, Joyce Slayton: *Your Job in the Computer Age: The Complete Guide to the Computer Skills You Will Need to Get the Job You Want*, Scribner, $8.95.

Monrissey, George: *Getting Your Act Together, Goal Setting for Fun, Health and Profit*, Wiley, $7.95.

Nassif, Janet Zhum: *Handbook of Health Careers*, Human Sciences Press, $9.95.

Nivens, Beatryce: *The Black Woman's Career Guide*, Anchor Press/ Doubleday, $12.95.

Noer, David: *How to Beat the Employment Game*, Ten Speed Press, $4.95.

Parker, Yana: *Damn Good Resume Guide*, Ten Speed Press, $4.95.

Peterson's Business and Management Jobs 1985, Peterson's Guides, $12.95.

Scheele, Adele: *Skills for Success*, Ballantine Books, $2.95.

Schenkel, Susan: *Giving Away Success*, McGraw-Hill, New York, $7.95.

Scott-Welch, Mary: *Networking: The Great New Way for Women to Get Ahead*, Warner Books, $2.50.

Shebar, Sharon Sigmond, and Judith Schoder: *How to Make Money at Home*, Simon & Schuster, $7.95.

Sheehy, Gail: *Path Finders*, Morrow, $15.95.

Uris, Auren, and John J. Tarrant: *Career Stages*, Seaview/Putnam, $15.95.

Wallace, Phyllis, with Linda Datchen and Julienne Malveaux: *Black Women in the Labor Force*, MIT Press, $16.00.

Weinstein, Robert U.: *Jobs for the 21st Century*, Collier Books, $6.95.

Wilbanks, Patricia M.: *How to Start a Typing Service in Your Own Home*, Arco, $5.00.

Wright, John W.: *The American Almanac of Jobs and Salaries*, Avon Books, $9.95.

Zimmerman, Caroline A.: *How to Break into the Media Professions*, Doubleday/Dolphin, $6.95.

Index

ABC Radio Spot Sales, 13
Academic credit, examinations
    and tests for, 281–286
Accredited Advisor in Insurance,
    241–242
ACT PEP tests, 282, 283, 287
Administrative assistants, skills
    used by, 41–43
Administrative Management
    Society, 195
Age, attitudes about, 20–21
Aims, 7
American Bar Association, 228,
    229
American College, 241
    Testing Program, 282, 287
American Council on Education,
    284, 286
American Dental Association,
    294

American Institute for Property
    and Liability Underwriters,
    241
American Medical Record
    Association, 291
American Occupational Therapy
    Association, 206, 207
American Physical Therapy
    Association, 203
American Society of Magazine
    Photographers, 224
American Society of Travel
    Agents, 106, 110, 235,
    236
Army Reserves, 9–10
Artists, commercial or graphic,
    219–222
    skills used by, 221–
    222
Ash, Mary Kay, 2

Association of Independent
    Colleges and Universities, 232
Association of Theatrical Press
    Agents and Managers, 10
Attitudes, 7–15
    about age, 20–21
    and conditioning, 7–8
Awards and honors, 102

Bachelor's degrees and programs,
    277–288
Baking, 57, 59
Bartenders, 296
Beauty careers, 254–257
Black Data Processing Associates,
    187, 191
*Black Woman's Career Guide,
    The* (Nivens), 40
Body reshapers, 201–205
Bookkeeping, 127–131, 296
Broadcast technicians, 295
Bronx Community College,
    272–274
Budget management, 127
Bureau of Labor Statistics, 187,
    189, 190, 216, 229, 255, 260,
    290–295, 297–299
Business cards, 72
Business machine repairers, 293
Business organizations, 305–306
Business owning, 262–267

Calligraphy, 57–58, 60
Capital, start-up, 264–265
Cards:
    business, 72
    calligraphy used in making of,
        57–58, 60
    card shops, 57–58, 60

Career:
    industry selection for,
        65–70
    workshops, 71
Career conferences, 71
Career course, plotting (*see*
    Plotting a career course)
Career Development Women's
    Studies, 287
Career dreams, 19–21, 58, 64
Carpenters, 297–298
Census Bureau, Department of
    Commerce, 2
Certifying Board of Legal
    Assistants, 228
Chartered Financial Consultant
    (ChFC), 241
Chartered Life Underwriter
    (CLU), 241
Chartered Property Casualty
    Underwriter (CPCU), 241
CLEP (College-Level
    Examination Program),
    281–283, 287
Cohen, Lisa, 14–15
College of Certified Planning,
    241
College credit by examination,
    281–286
College education records:
    degrees and programs, 271–288
    no degree, 99–100, 124, 129,
        136
College of Insurance, 241
College-Level Examination
    Program (CLEP), 281–283,
    287
Commercial artists and designers,
    219–222

Commission of Dental
  Accreditation, 209–210
Commission on Opticianry
  Accreditation, 213
Communications, 65–66,
  131–136, 155–157
Community colleges, 272–277
Computer field, 164–168, 185–192
  on-the-job training, 186, 190
Computer operators, skills used
  by, 191–192
Computer service technicians,
  skills used by, 187–188
Conditioning and attitudes, 7–8
Conferences, career, 71
Conventions, professional
  associations, 71
Cooks and chefs, 297
Correspondence schools,
  280–281, 283–284
Cosmetiques, 2
Cosmetologists, 254–257
  skills used by, 256–257
Council of National Organizations
  for Adult Education,
  286
Court reporters, 231–233
  skills used by, 233
Cover letters for résumés,
  151–160
Creative careers, 219–226,
  254–257

Daley, Hope, 11
Dancer and Fitzgerald
  (advertising agency), 12
DANTES (Defense Activity for
  Non-Traditional Education
  Support), 281–283, 287

DANTES Subject Standardized
  Tests (DSSTs), 282
Defense Activity for Non-
  Traditional Education
  Support (DANTES),
  281–283, 287
Dental assistants, 208–211
  skills used by, 211
Dental laboratory technicians,
  294
Department of Commerce,
  Census Bureau, 2
*Dictionary of Occupational
  Titles* (DOT), 40, 43, 44,
  116, 146
Diet Center, 2
Disc jockies, 58, 60
Dispensing optician, 212–215
DOT (Dictionary of Occupational
  Titles), 40, 43, 44, 116, 146
Drafters, 295
DSSTs (DANTES Subject
  Standardized Tests), 282

Earth Wind and Fire (singing
  group), 10
Educational Testing Service,
  286
Electrical workers, 298
Embalmers, 290–291
Emergency medical technicians,
  215–218
Employment agencies, 78–80
*Encyclopedia of Associations,
  The,* 64
Engineering and science
  technicians, 293
Entertainment publicists,
  10–11

Entrepreneurial careers, 262–267
Environment, work, 70
Essence, 13–14
Examinations and tests for
    academic credit, 281–286

Fact-finding interviews, 74–77
Ferguson, Sybil, 2
Fields, Debbi, 2
File clerks, skills used by, 45–46,
    166–167
Flight attendants, 294–295
Flower arrangements, 58, 59
Fund-raising skills, 51–52, 101
Funeral directors, 290–291

Gale Research Company, 64
Gandy, Irene, 10–11
Giugni, June, 2
Goals and plotting, 16–23
    monetary goals, 21–23
Graduate Record Examination,
    281, 282, 287
Graduate school, eligibility for,
    285
Graphic designers, artists,
    219–222

Hamburger Hamlet, 2
Health careers, 197–218
High school courses and records,
    98–99
High-technology careers, 185–196
    degrees, 285
Hotel management, 258–261
*How to Get Credit for What You
    Have Learned as a
    Homemaker or Volunteer*,
    286

Independent study, 280–281
Industry designations:
    Accredited Advisor in
        Insurance, 241–242
    ChFC (Chartered Financial
        Consultant), 241
    CLU (Chartered Life
        Underwriter), 241
    CPCU (Chartered Property
        Casualty Underwriter), 241
Industry selection for career,
    65–70
Information processing,
    192–196
Institute of Certified Travel
    Agents, 235
Insurance agents and brokers,
    116, 239–245
    skills used by, 116, 243–245
Interests and career potential,
    57–62, 65–66
    tabulation, 59–62
Interviews:
    for employment, 99, 160–181
        after-interview manners,
            180–181
        clothes to wear, 169, 176
        dos and don'ts, 175–177
        failure, reasons for, 174
        manner(s), 170–174, 180–181
        mistakes to avoid, 170–171
        preparation for, 160–170,
            173–174
        questions: frequent, 161–163
            typical, tackling, 163–168
        rapport and ice-breaking,
            170
        relocation, 179–180
        salary negotiation, 178–179

Interviews: for employment (*Cont.*):
  types of, 171–174
    group, 172–173
    question and answer, 171–172
    successive, 173
    unstructured, 172
  fact-finding, 74–77

Job interviews (*see* Interviews, for employment)
Jobs, list of, 301–304
Journal of Emergency Medical Services, 216, 217
Junior colleges, 272–277

Katz, Lillian, 2
KGO Newstalk Radio, San Francisco, 12–13

LaBelle (singing group), 10
Labor Unions (organization), 64
LaGuardia Community College, 274–276
Lathrop Village Volunteers of the Community, 105, 107, 109
Legal assistants, 227–230
  skills used by, 230
Leisure careers, 258–261
Lens workers, 212–215
Lewis, Ed, 13
Lewis, Marilyn, 2
Life Underwriter Training Council (LUTC), 241
Lillian Vernon, 2
Lithographers, 299
LUTC (Life Underwriter Training Council), 241

McPhearson, Carolyn, 8–9, 101
Manufacturers' salespeople, 250–253
  skills used by, 252–253
Market research, 263
Mary Kay Cosmetics, 2
Marymount Manhattan College, 277–279
Media research, 12–13
Medical record technicians and clerks, 291
Medical technicians, emergency, 215–218
  skills used by, 217–218
Middle States Association of Colleges and Schools, 283–285
Minority Business Development Agency, 262
Mrs. Fields' Cookies, 2
Monetary goals, 21–23
Morgan Stanley, 11
Morris, June, 2
Morris Travel, 2
Motel management, 258–261

National Association of Dental Assistants, 210
National Association of Health Underwriters, 241
National Association of Legal Assistants, 228, 229
National Association of Realtors, 248, 250
National Association of Secretaries, 102
National Federation of Licensed Practical Nurses, 199

National Guide to Educational Credit for Training Programs, 286

National Home Study Council, 281

National League of Nursing, 283, 285

National Secretaries Association International, 40

National Shorthand Reporters Association, 232

National Trade and Professional Associations of the United States and Canada, 64

National University Extension Association (NUEA), 280–281

guide to correspondence study, 281

Nequai Cosmetics, 13

Networking, 70–77, 175, 179

New York National Program on Noncollegiate Sponsored Instruction (PONSI), 284

New York State Board of Regents, 283

Nightingale, Florence, 197

Northwestern Lindquist Endicott Report, The, 163, 174

NUEA (National University Extension Association), 280–281

NUEA Guide to Independent Study through Correspondence Instruction, 281

Nurses, 197–201

licensed practical, skills used by, 200–201

Nurses' training programs, 199

Occupational Outlook Handbook Quarterly, 194, 199, 201, 203, 206, 210, 220, 221, 232, 242, 248, 252, 256, 259

Occupational therapy assistants, 205–208

skills used by, 207–208

Office of Educational Credit, 286

Office helpers, skills used by, 47–48

Ohio University Course Credit by Examination, 283

100 Best Companies to Work for in America, The (Levering, Moskowitz & Katz), 70

Operating room technicians, 292

Opticians, dispensing, 212–215

skills used by, 214–215

Optometric assistants, 292

Photographers, skills used by, 224–226

Photographic laboratory workers, 299

Photography, 222–226

Physical therapist assistants, 201–205

skills used by, 204–205

Plotting a career course, 16–23, 63–80

and employment agencies, 78–80

fact-finding interviews, 74–77

industry selecting, 65–70

information gathering, 63–65, 70

monetary goals, 21–23

and networking, 70–77

Plotting a career course (*Cont.*):
and want ads, 78–80
and work environment, 70
worksheets, 16–23
Plumbers and pipe fitters, 297
PONSI (Programs on
Noncollegiate Sponsored
Instruction), 284
Powell, Claudia, 9–10
Printers and lithographers,
299
Professional groups, 102
Professional Secretaries
Association International,
194
Profiles of successful people,
72
Programs on Noncollegiate
Sponsored Instruction
(PONSI), 284
Public relations, 8–9, 14, 58, 60,
122–127
skills required for, 53–55, 101,
116
Publicists, entertainment, 10–11
Purchasing, 9–10

Radiologic technologists, 292–293
RCEs (Regents College
Examinations), 281–283,
287
Real estate agents and brokers,
245–250
specialties, 246–248
Referral cover letters, 154–155
Regents College Degree
Program, 283–285, 287
Regents College Examinations
(RCEs), 281–283, 287

Registered Health Underwriters,
241
Relocation, 179–180
Respiratory therapy workers, 294
Response-to-posting cover letter,
155–159
Résumés, 80–151
action words, 114–115
analysis worksheet, 149–150
appearance of, 150–151
assembling, 111–116
"before" and "after," 117–144
checklist, dos and don't,
144–148
chronological, 103–104, 108,
112–113, 132, 144–146
combination, 108–110, 116,
147–148
cover letters, 151–160
functional, 104–108, 116, 132,
146–147
job duties, emphasizing,
141–144
mistakes, avoiding, 117–144
preliminary analysis, 82–102
relevant material, 81–82
types of, 102–110
Retail trade sales workers, 290
Riperton, Minnie, 10

Salary negotiations, 178–179
Sales careers, 239–253
insurance, 239–245
manufactured goods, 250–253
real estate, 245–250
retail trade, 290
Sales clerks, skills used by, 49–50
SBA (Small Business
Administration), 262, 265

Schools, types of:
    community colleges,
      272–277
    correspondence, 280–281,
      283–284
    graduate, eligibility for, 285
    junior colleges, 272–277
    vocational, 100
SCORE, 265
Secretarial training, 11
Secretarial work and skills, 24–25,
    38–40, 137–140, 296
Skills, 24–56, 100, 101
    checklist, 25–36
    secretarial, 24–25, 38–40,
      137–140, 296
    used by administrative
      assistants, 41–43
    used by artists, commercial or
      graphic, 221–222
    used by computer operators,
      191–192
    used by computer service
      technicians, 187–188
    used by cosmetologists, 256–257
    used by court reporters, 233
    used by dental assistants, 211
    used by emergency medical
      technicians, 217–218
    used by entrepreneurs,
      266–267
    used by file clerks, 45–46,
      166–167
    used by fund-raisers, 51–52, 101
    used by hotel or motel
      managing assistants,
      260–261
    used by insurance agents and
      brokers, 116, 243–245

Skills (*Cont.*):
    used by legal assistants, 230
    used by licensed practical
      nurses, 200–201
    used by manufacturers'
      salespeople, 252–253
    used by occupational therapy
      assistants, 207–208
    used by office helpers, 47–48
    used by opticians, 214–215
    used by photographers,
      224–226
    used by physical therapist
      assistants, 204–205
    used by public-relations
      specialists, 53–55, 101,
      116
    used by real estate agents and
      brokers, 249–250
    used by sales clerks, 49–50
    used by travel agents, 236–
      238
    used by typists, 44, 100
    used by word processing
      specialists, 195–196
    worksheet for recognizing, 37
Small Business Administration
    (SBA), 262, 265
Social service aides, 290
State employment agencies, 79
State University of New York
    (SUNY), 287
Stenographers, 296
Stenotype Institute, 232
Study, independent, 280–281
Stumbling blocks to careers,
    20–21
SUNY (State University of New
    York), 287

Task Force of Volunteer
Accreditation, 286
Taylor, Shana, 14
Taylor, Susan, 13–14
Teacher aide field, 291
Technology, degrees in, 285
Technology careers, high-,
185–196
TenEyck, Rose, 12–13
Tests and examinations for
academic credit, 281–286
Theatrical publicists, 10–11
Thomas A. Edison College,
285–286
Trade magazines, 72
Travel, 102
Travel agents, 105–110,
234–238
skills used by, 236–238
Typists, skills used by, 44, 100
(*See also* Secretarial work and
skills)

Underwriters, insurance, 116,
239–245
U.S. Armed Forces Institute,
282
U.S. Department of Labor, 116,
187, 189, 190, 194, 216, 221,
229, 255, 260, 290–295,
297–299
U.S. Department of Trans-
portation, 216

University End-of-Course
Examinations, 281, 283
University of North Carolina
Independent Study, 283
University of North Carolina
School of Dentistry, 209–210

Vocational schools and training,
100
Volunteers' skills, credit for,
286

Want-ad cover letters, 155–159
Want ads, 78–80
Women, career workshops for,
71
Women in Communications
(professional association), 65,
136
Women's business organizations,
305–306
Women's magazines, 71–72
Word processing specialists,
158–159, 164–168, 179,
192–196
certificate programs for, 274
learning the job, 193–194
Word Processing World,
158–159
Work environment, 70
Workshops, career, 71

X-ray technologists, 292–293

Catalog

If you are interested in a list of fine Paperback
books, covering a wide range of subjects
and interests, send your name and address,
requesting your free catalog, to:

McGraw-Hill Paperbacks
11 West 19th Street
New York, N.Y. 10011